this is coffee

Robbie Orbie

I have measured out my life
with coffee spoons.

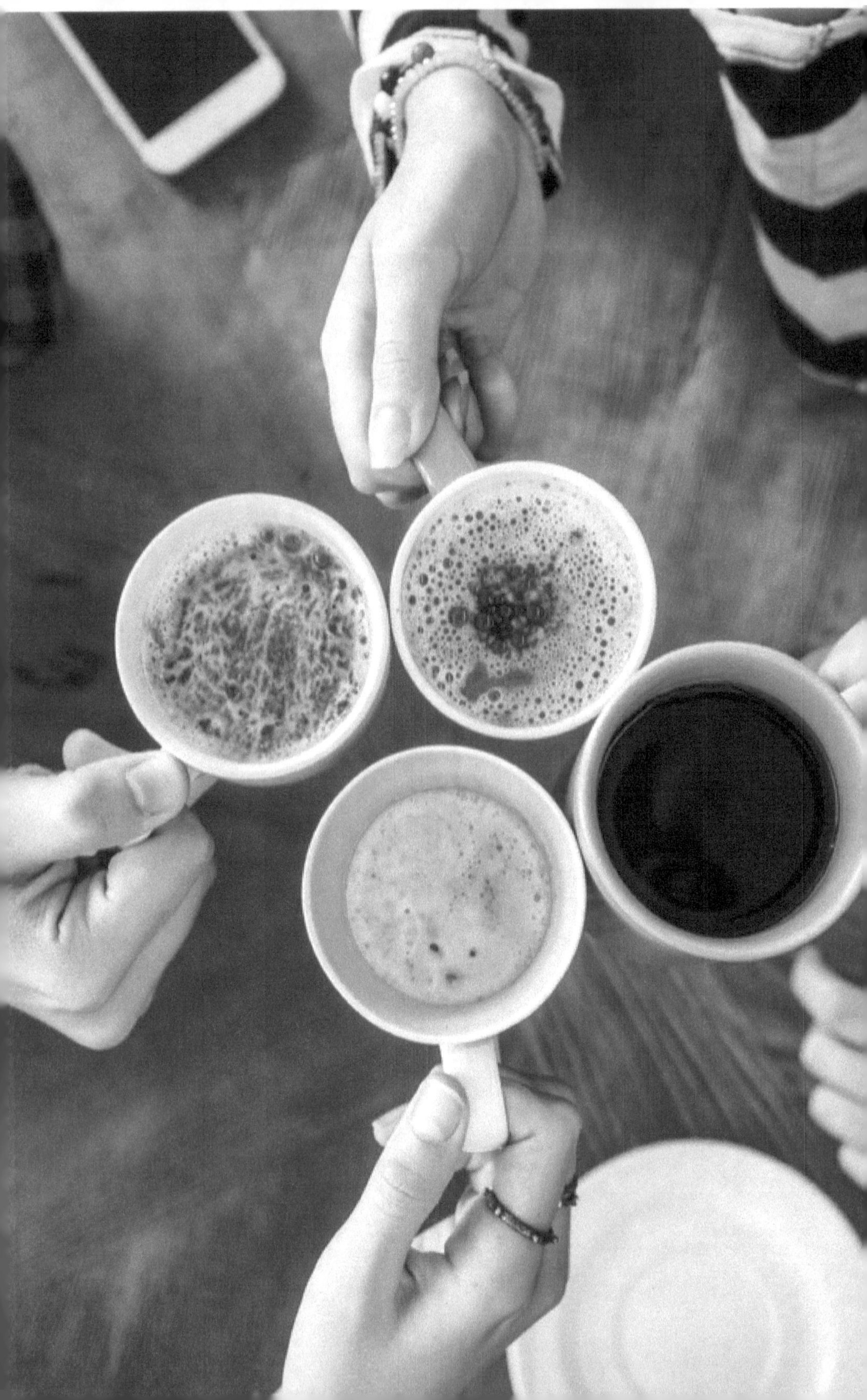

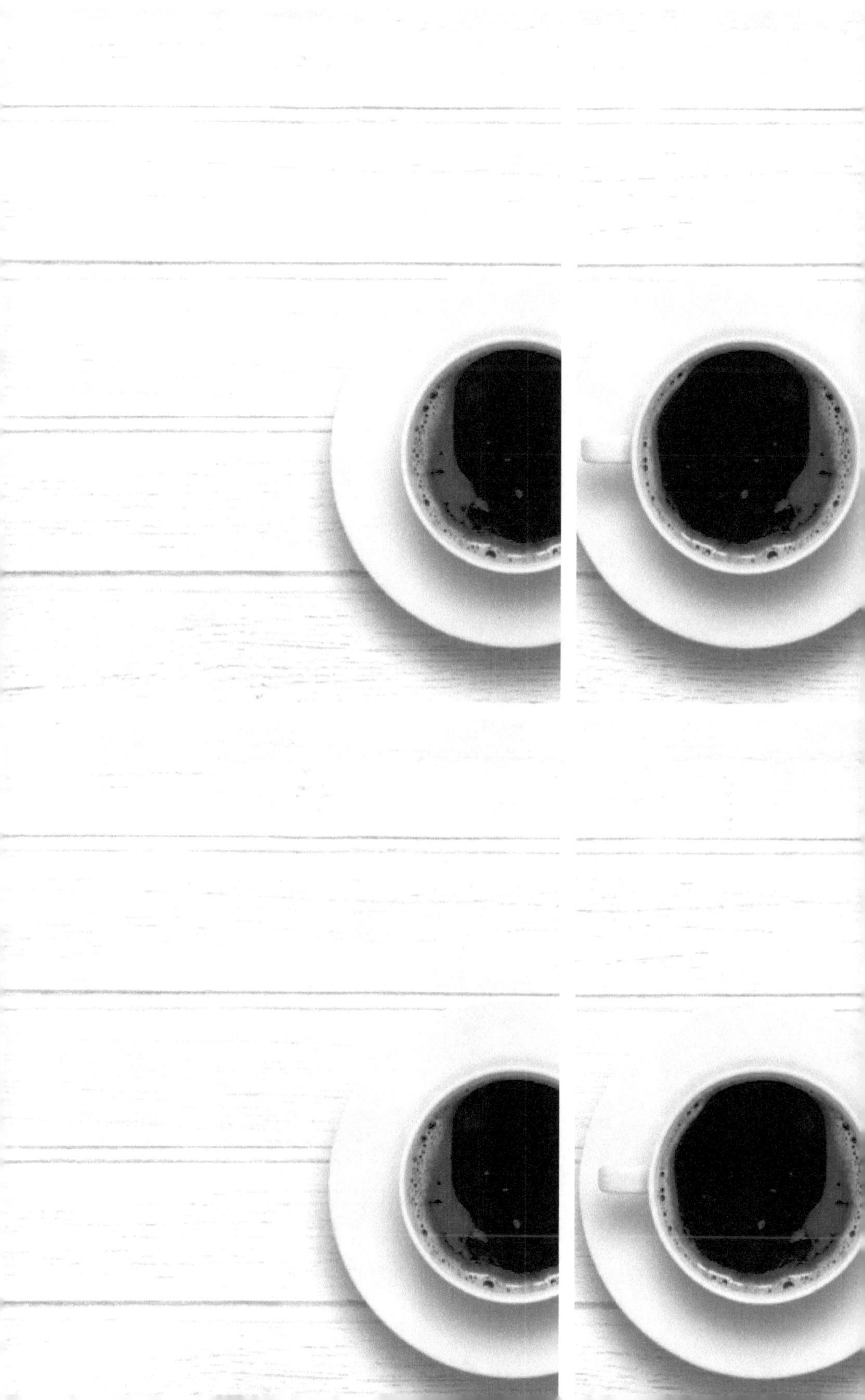

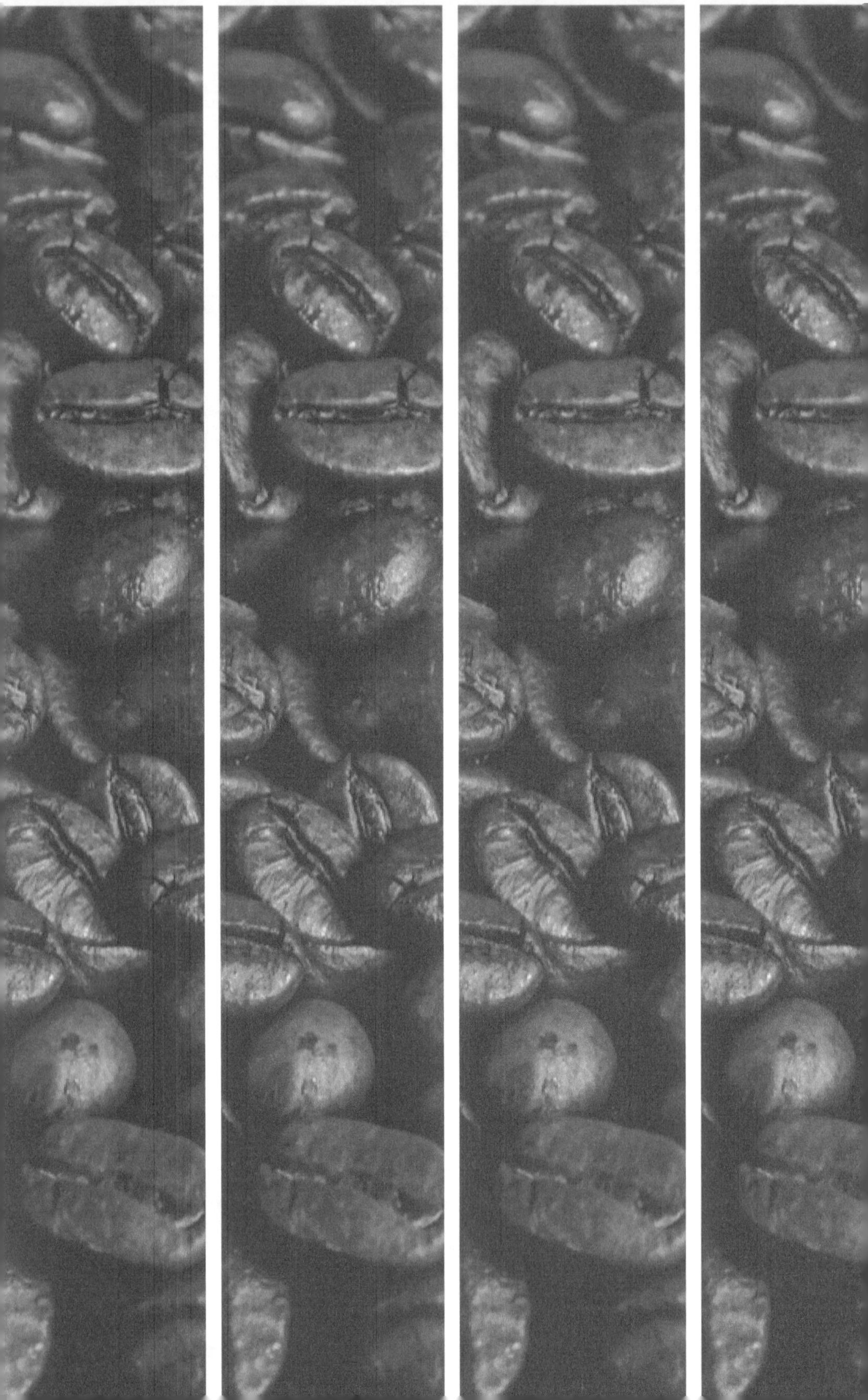

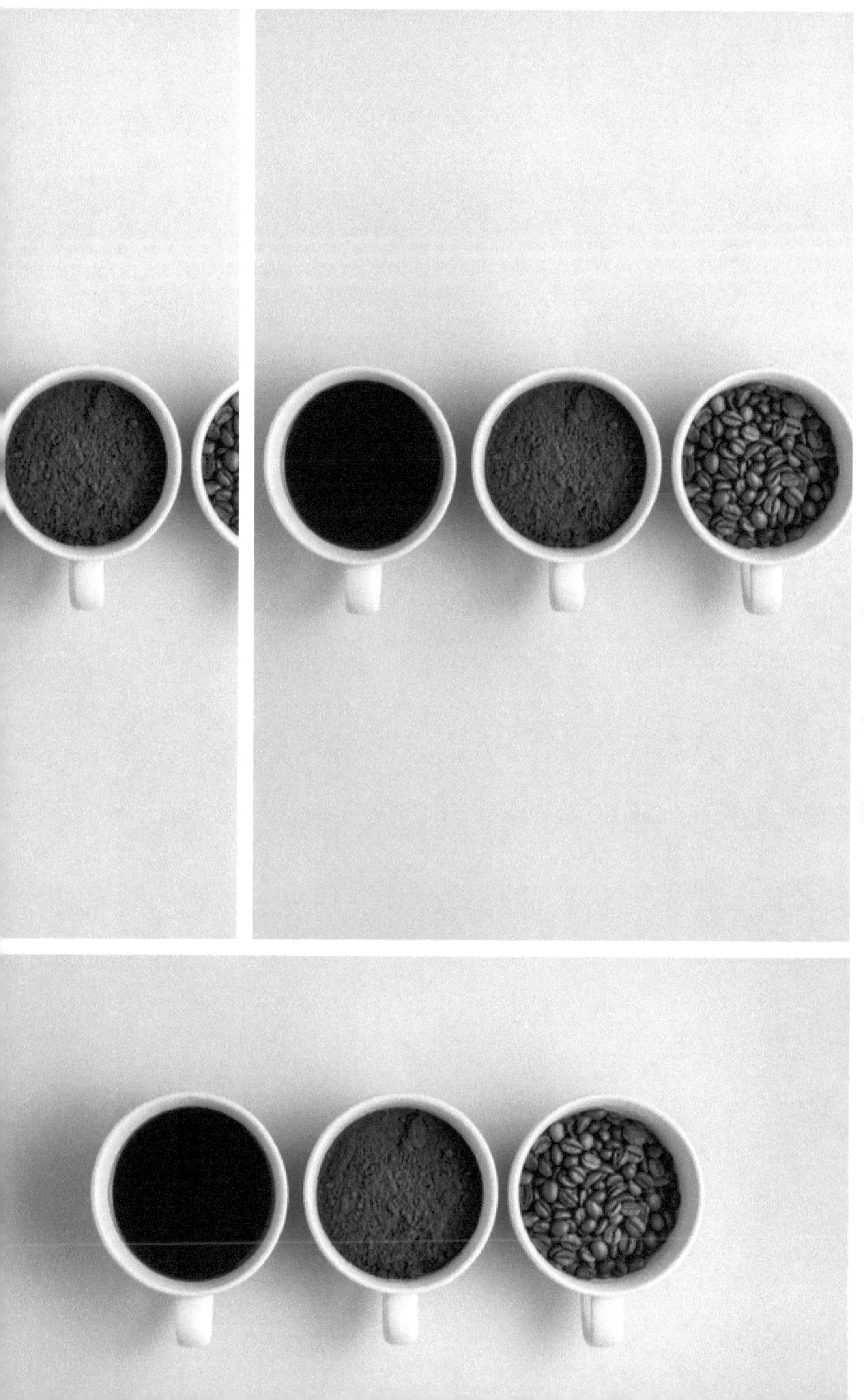

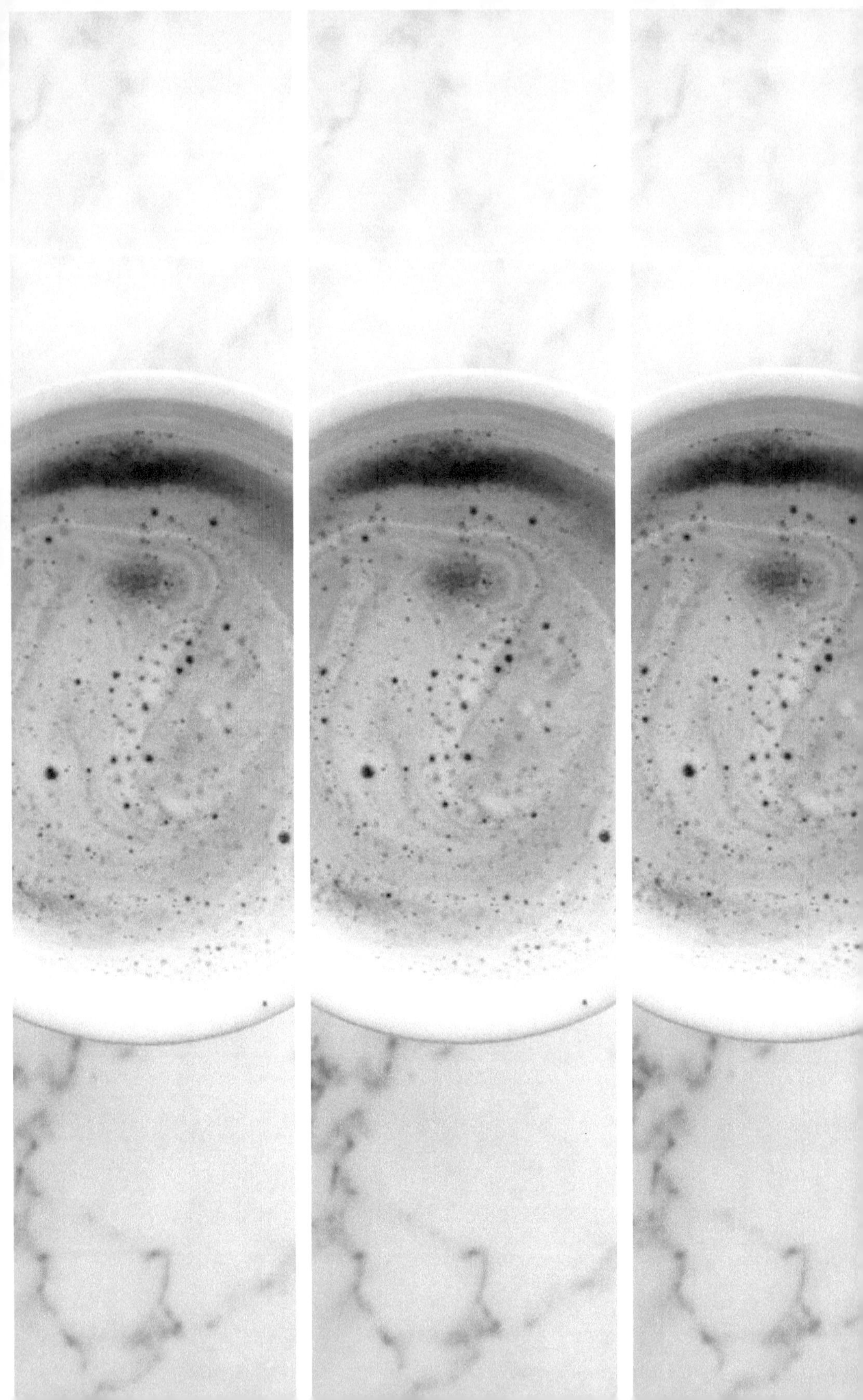

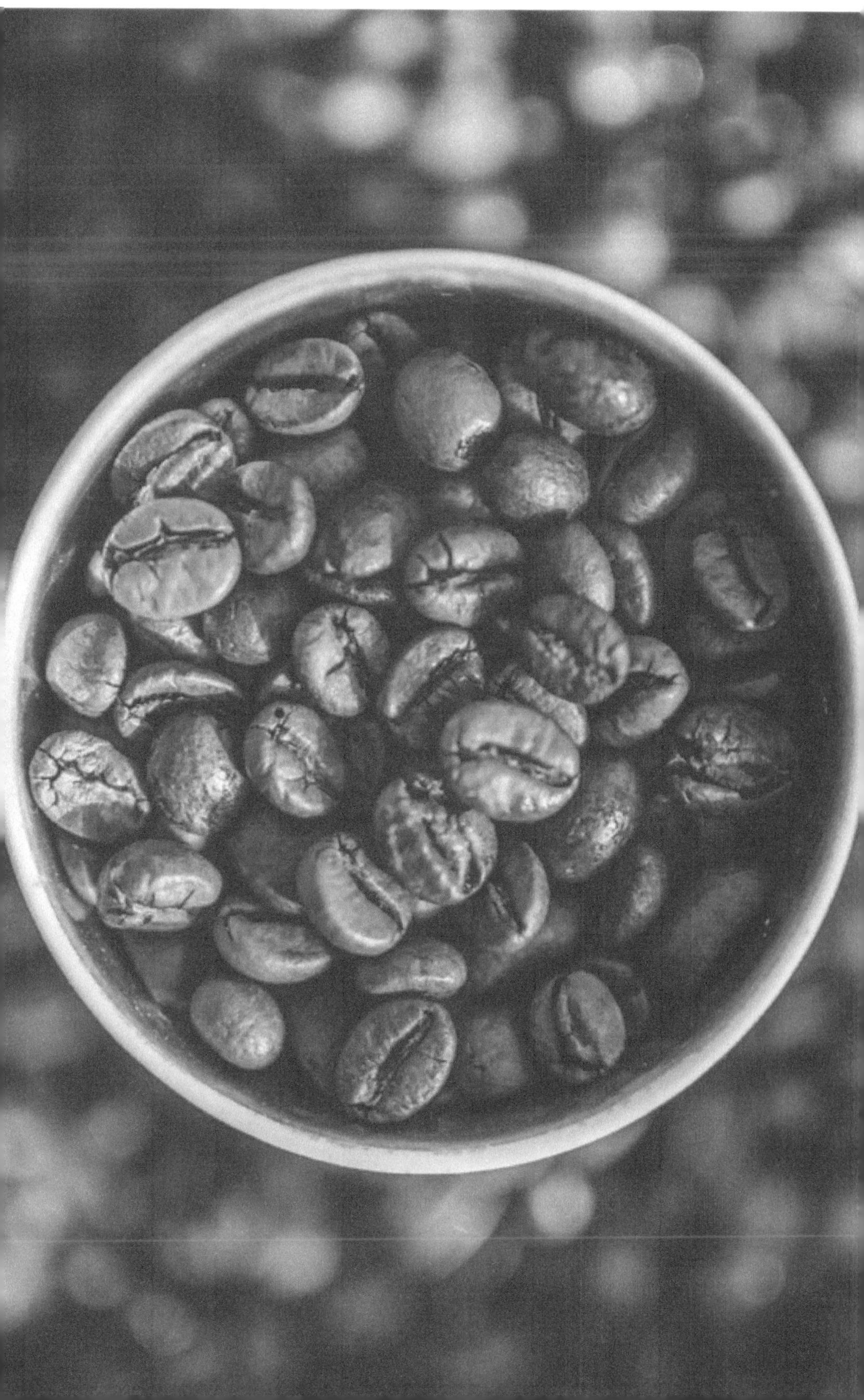

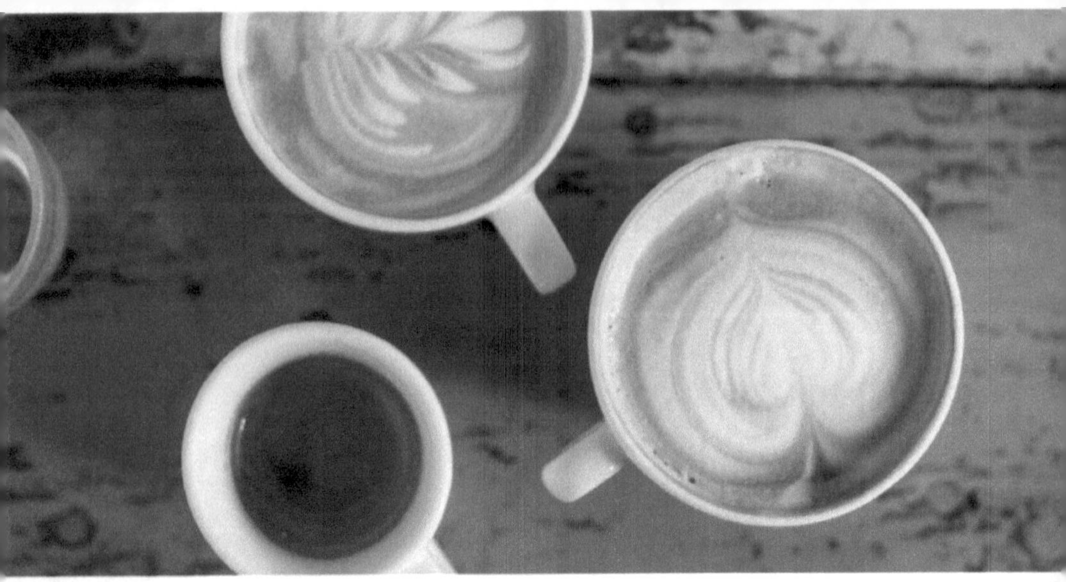

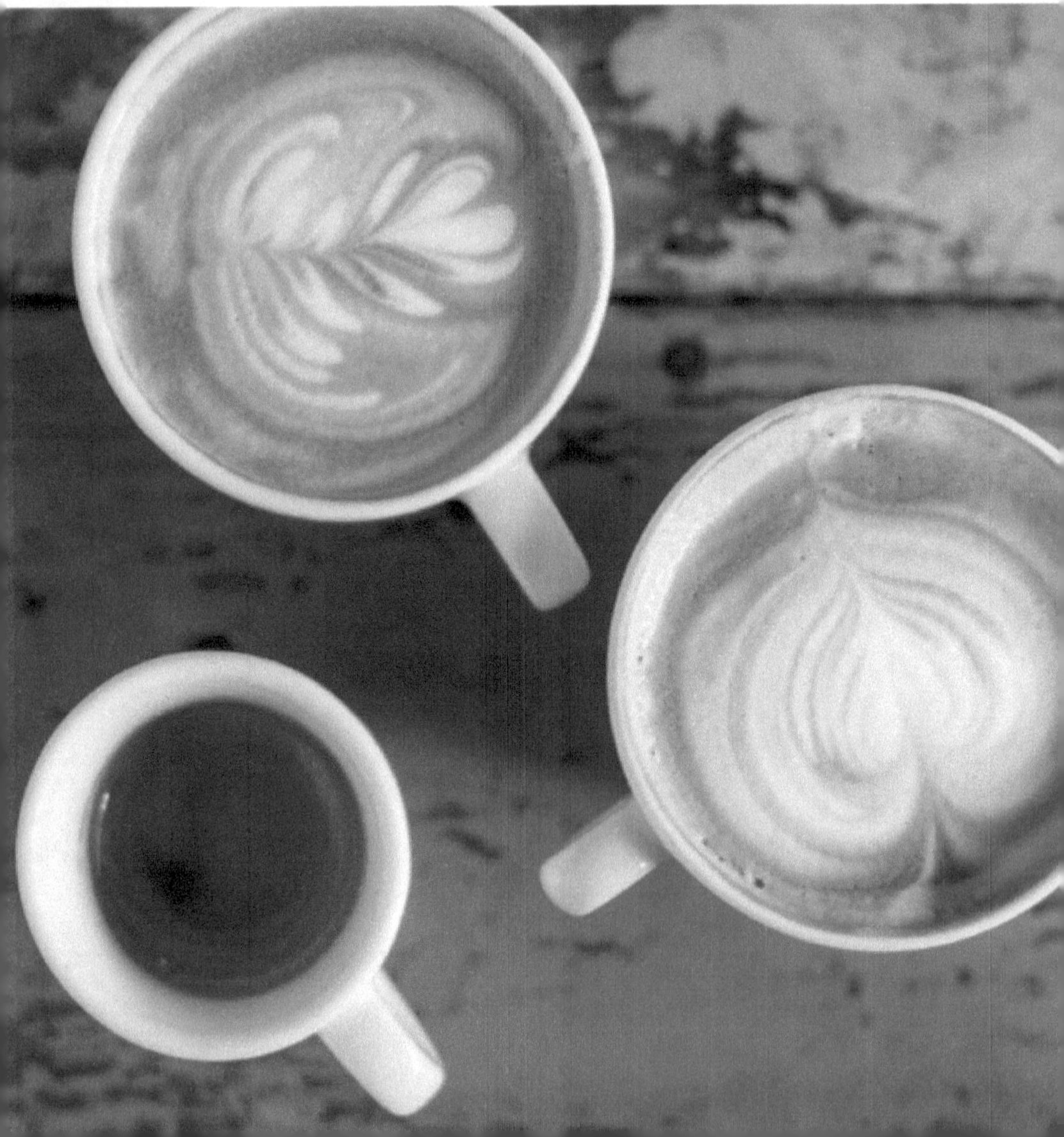

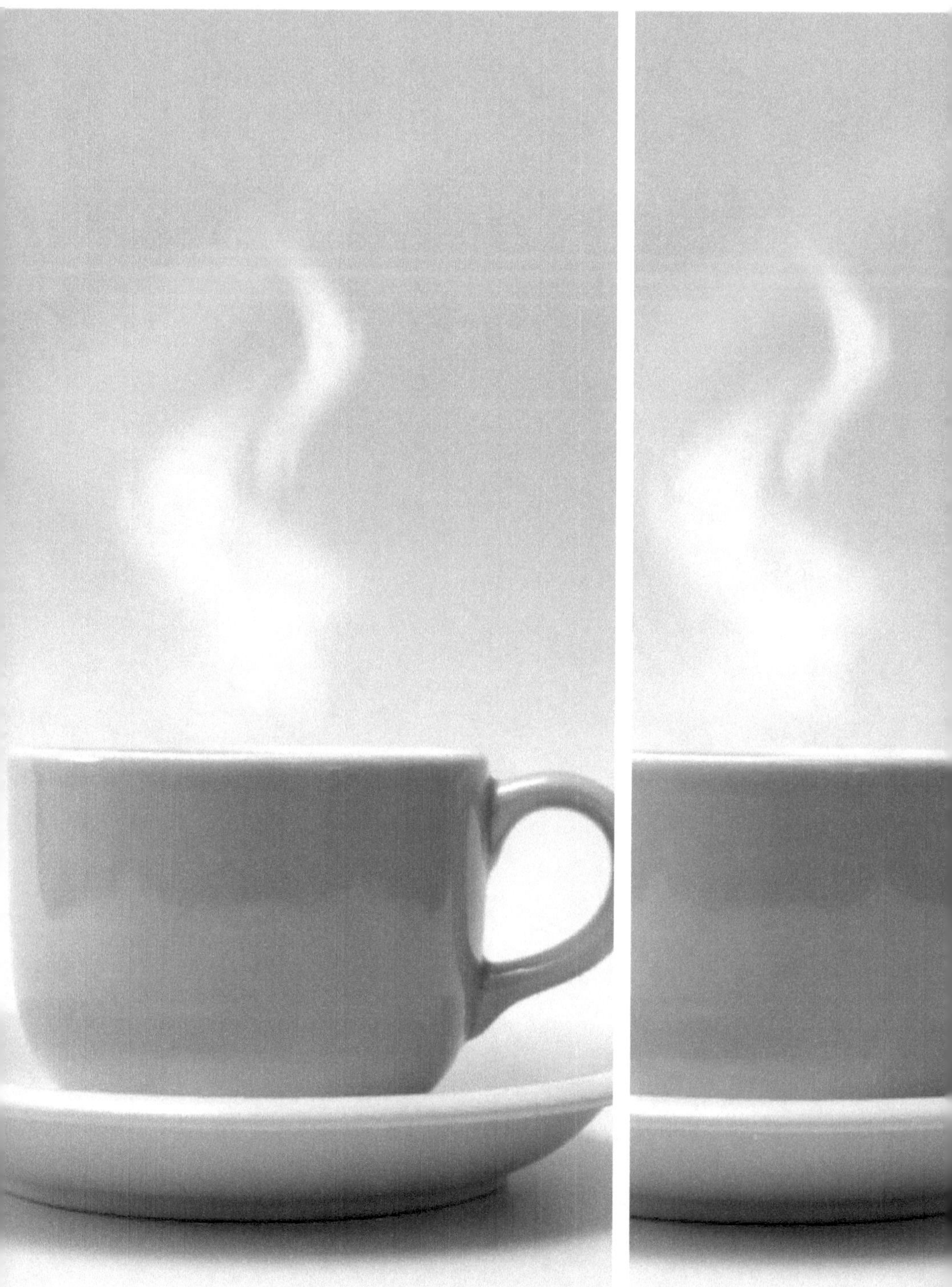

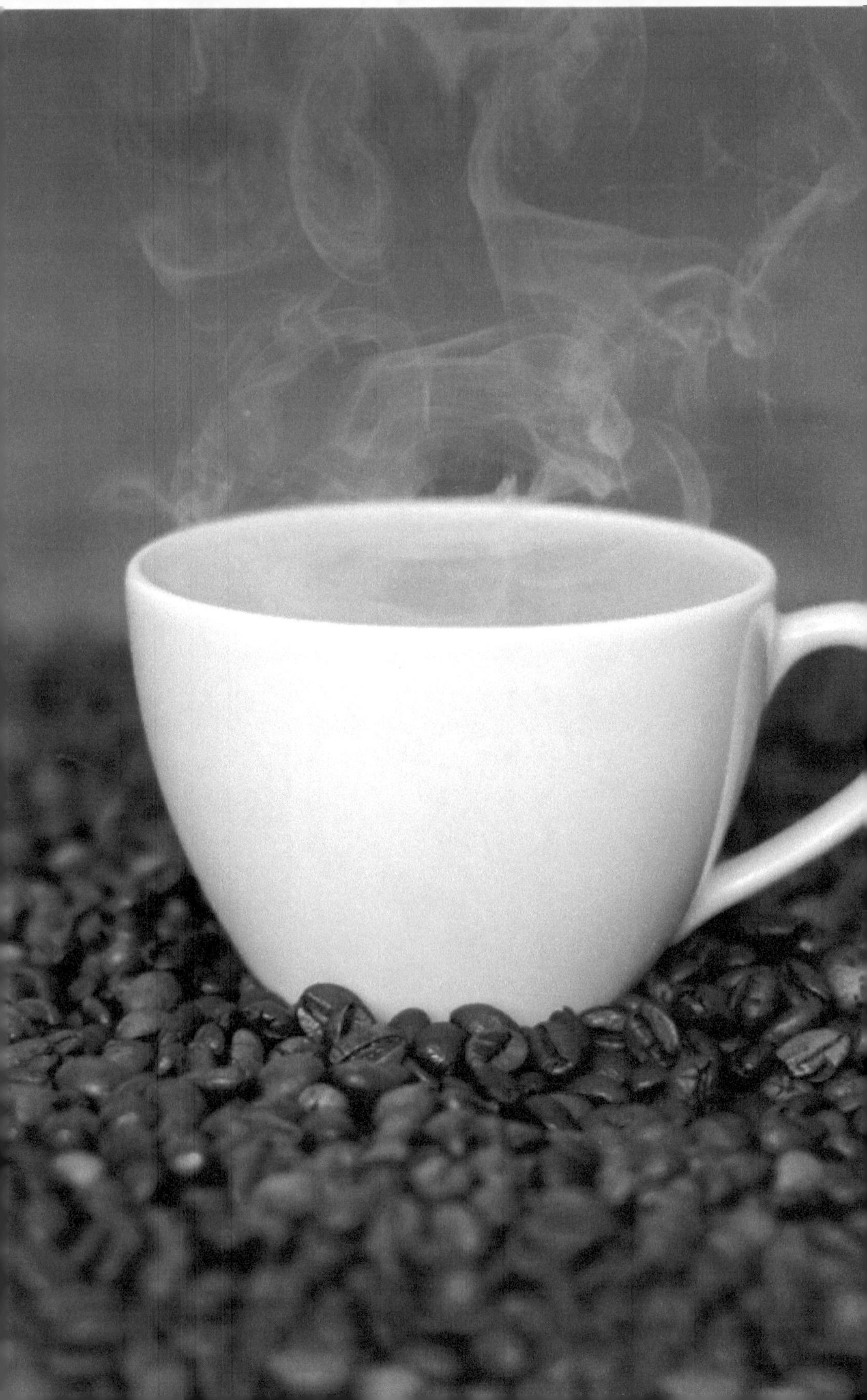

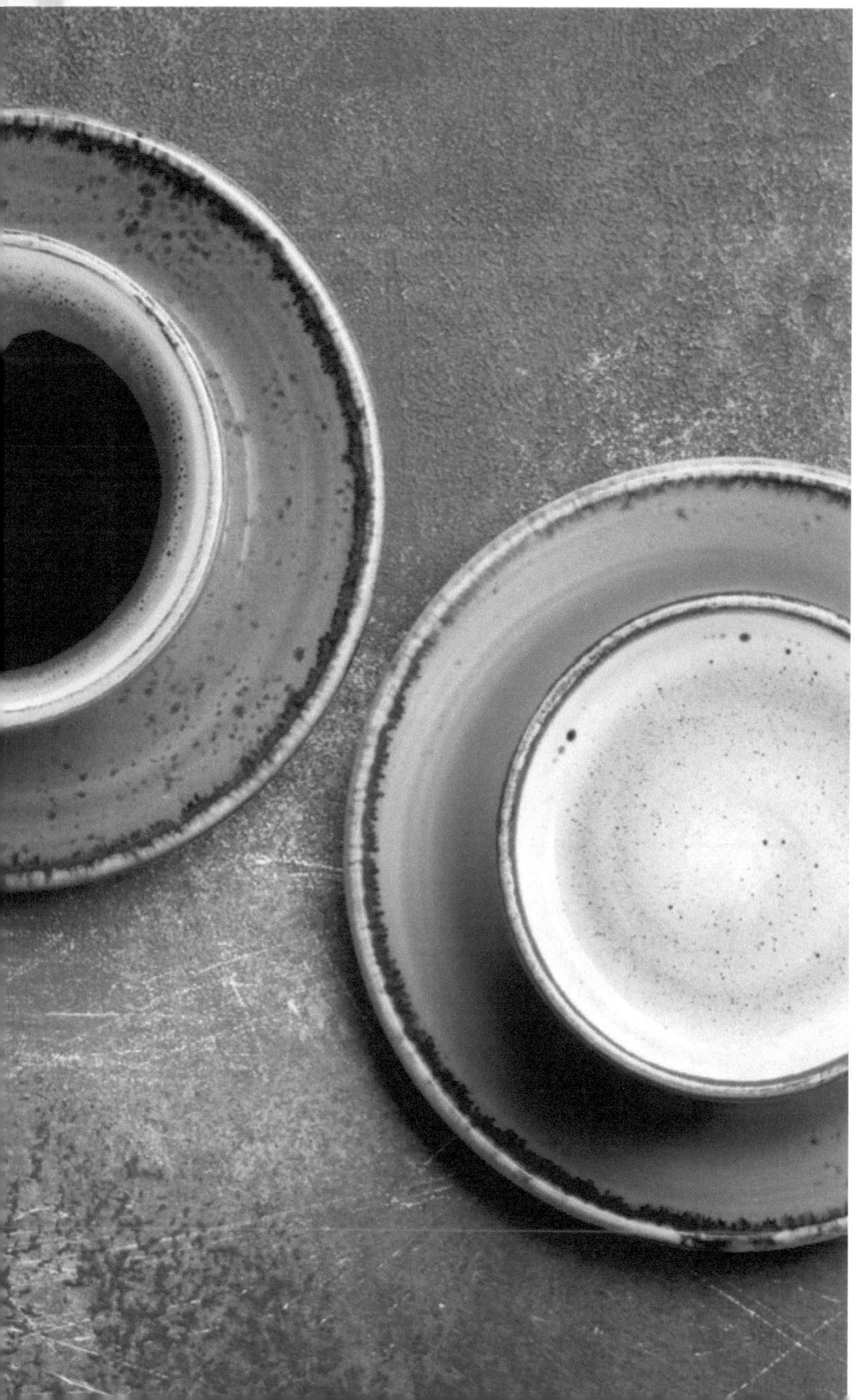

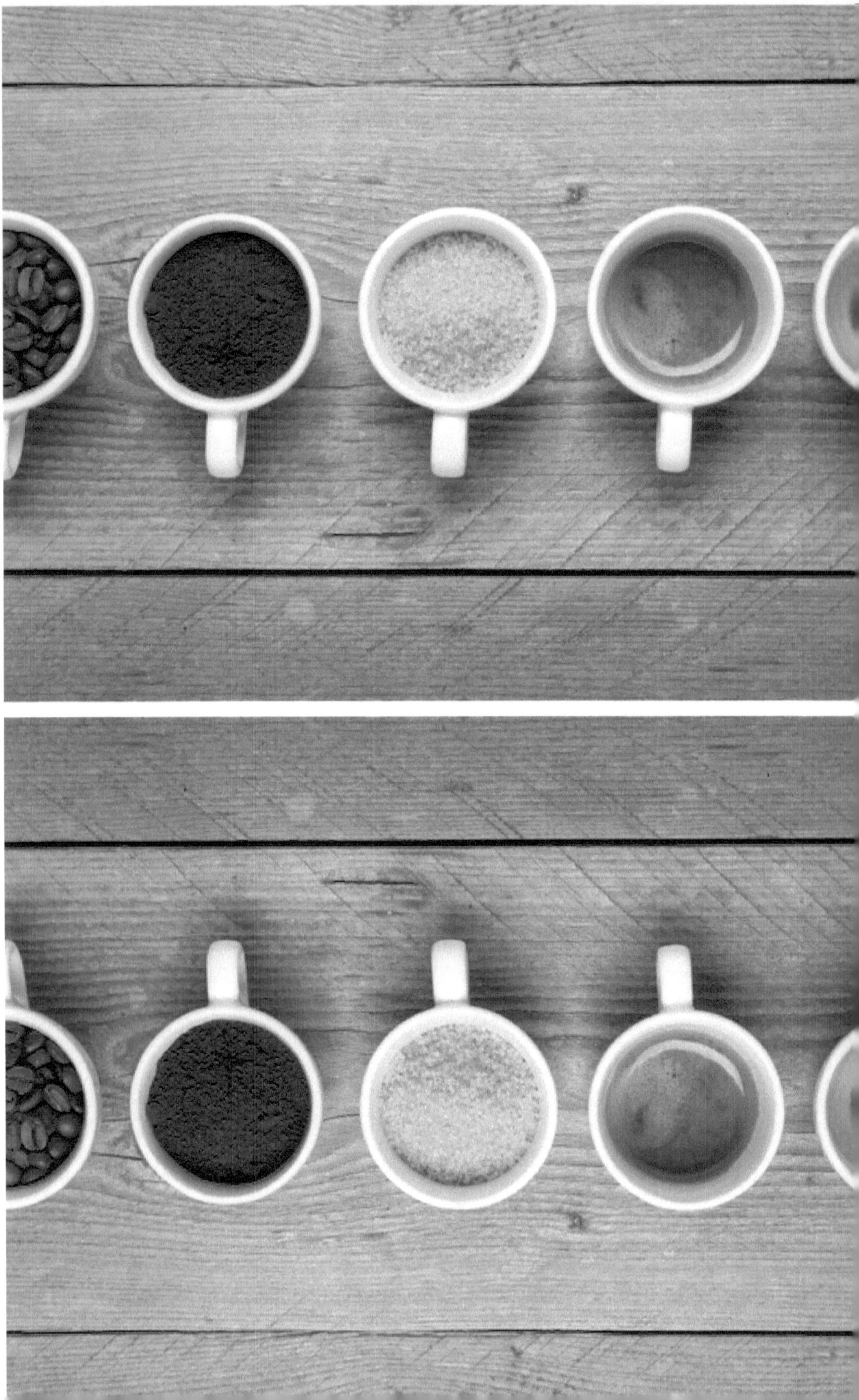

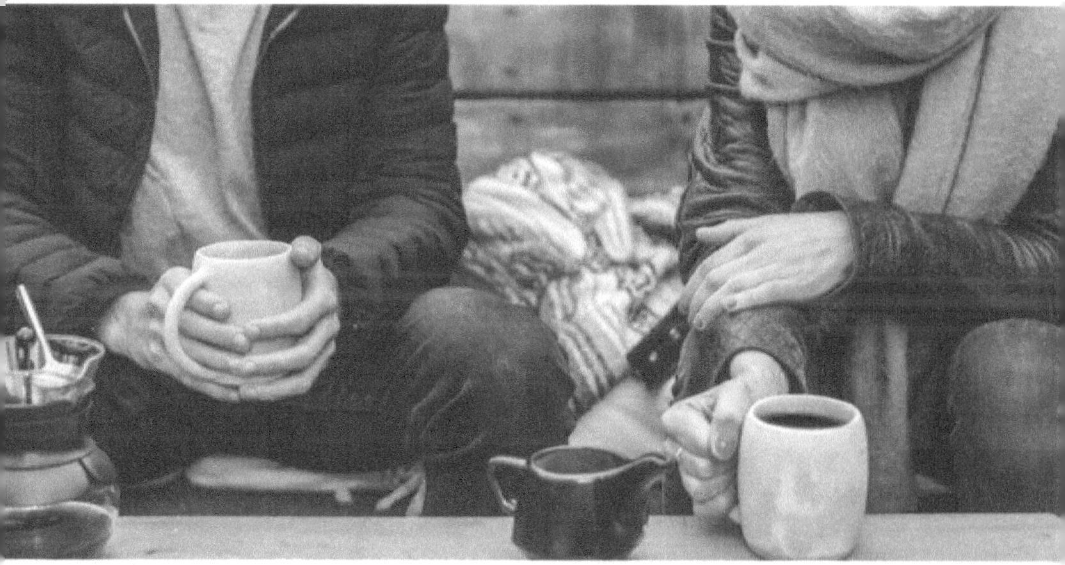
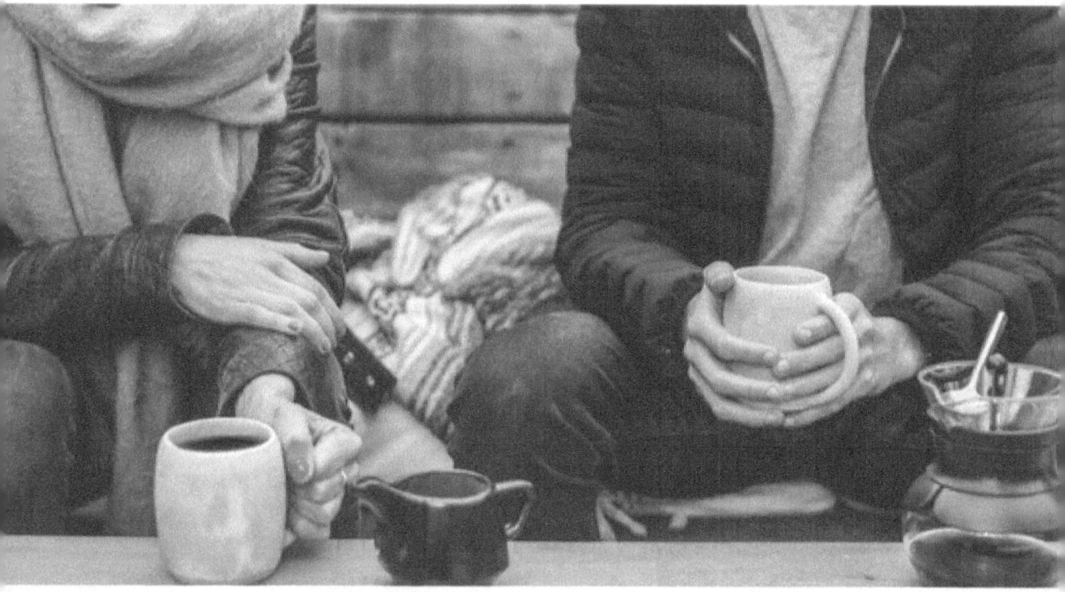
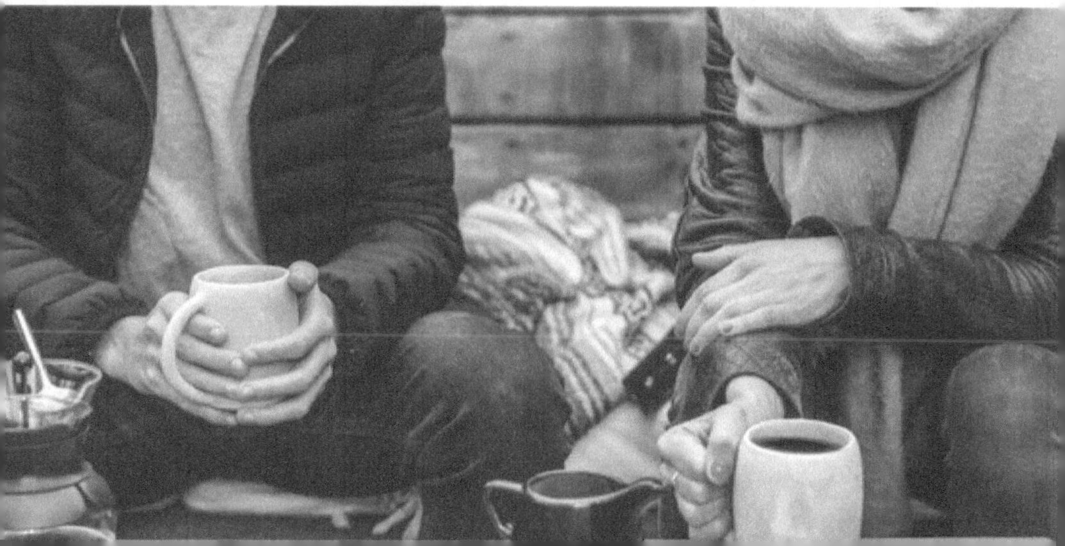

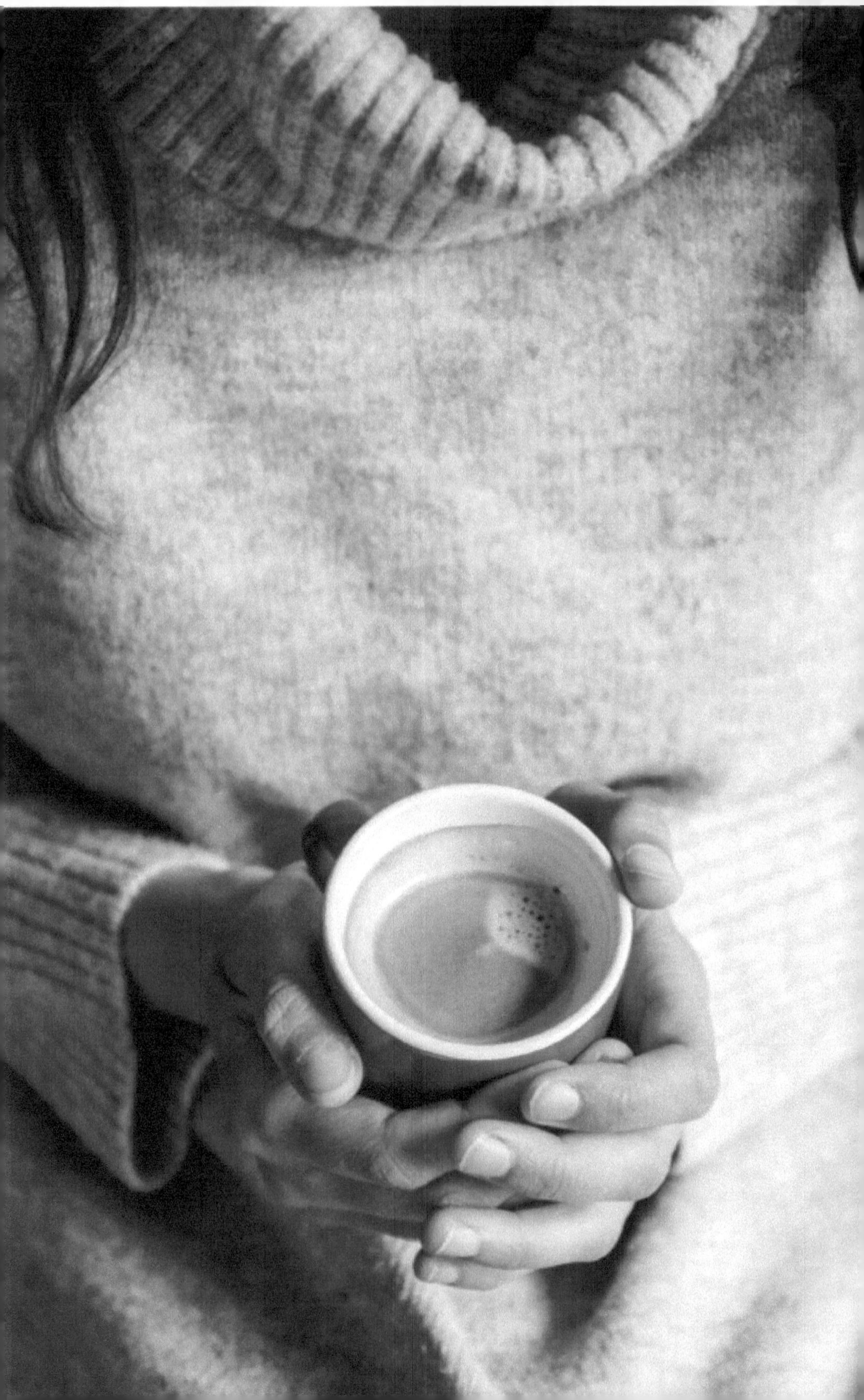

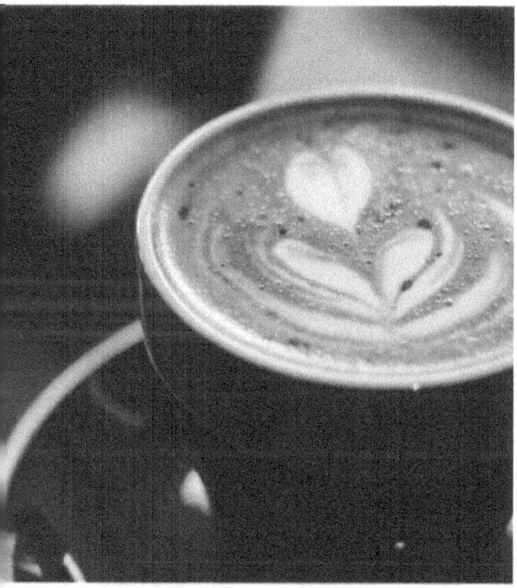
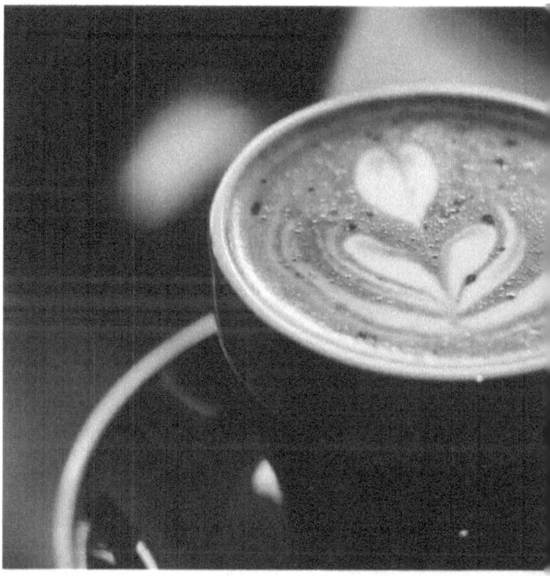
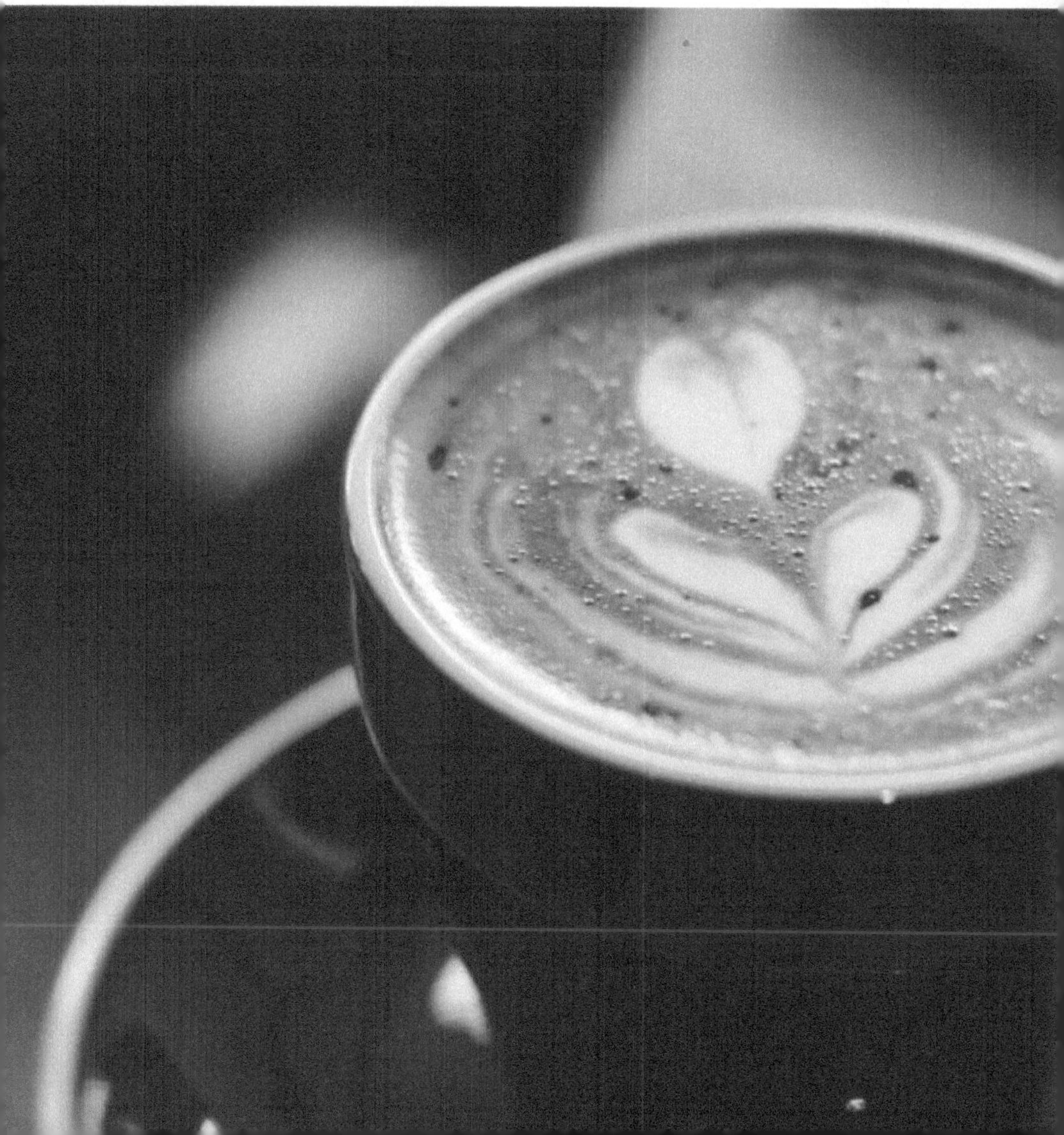

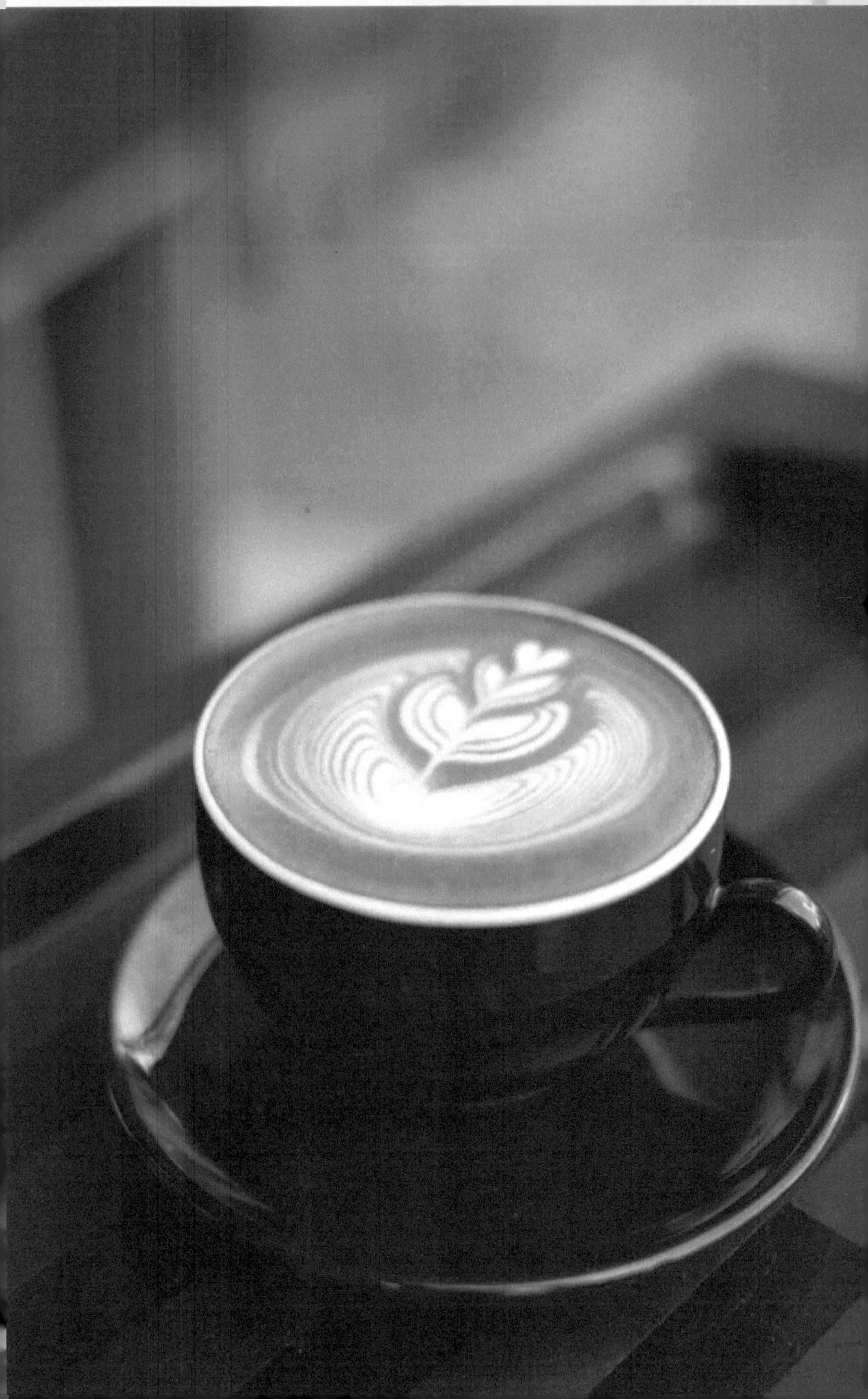

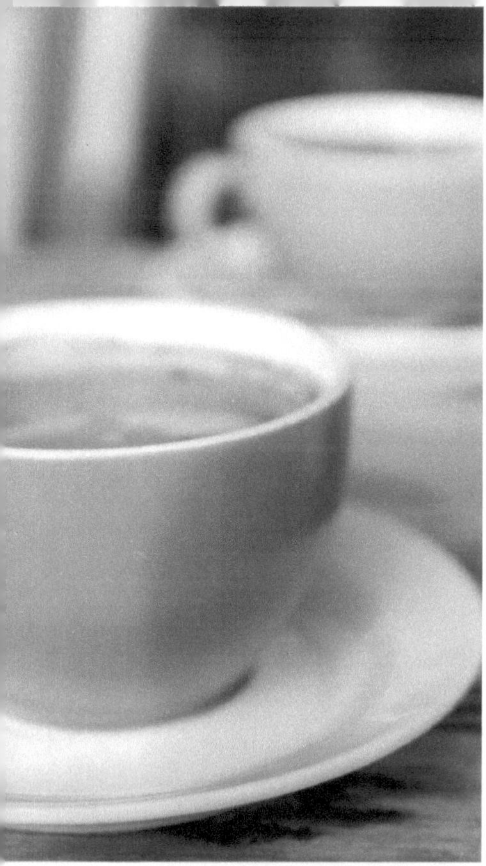
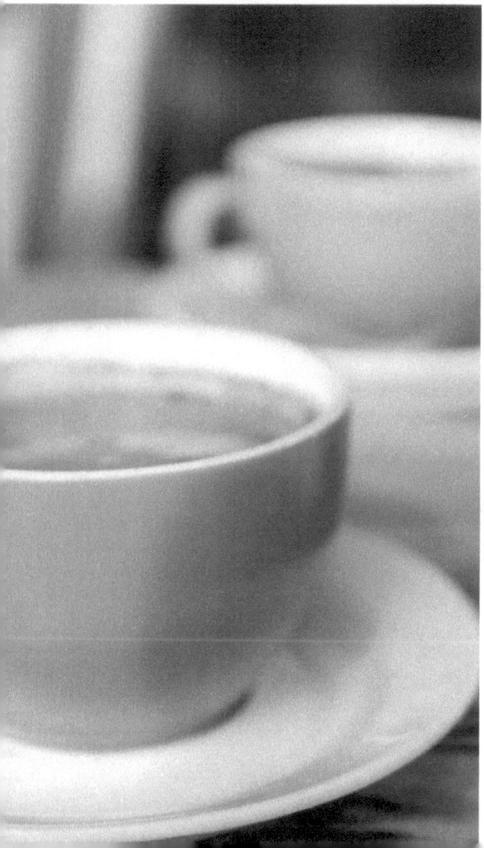
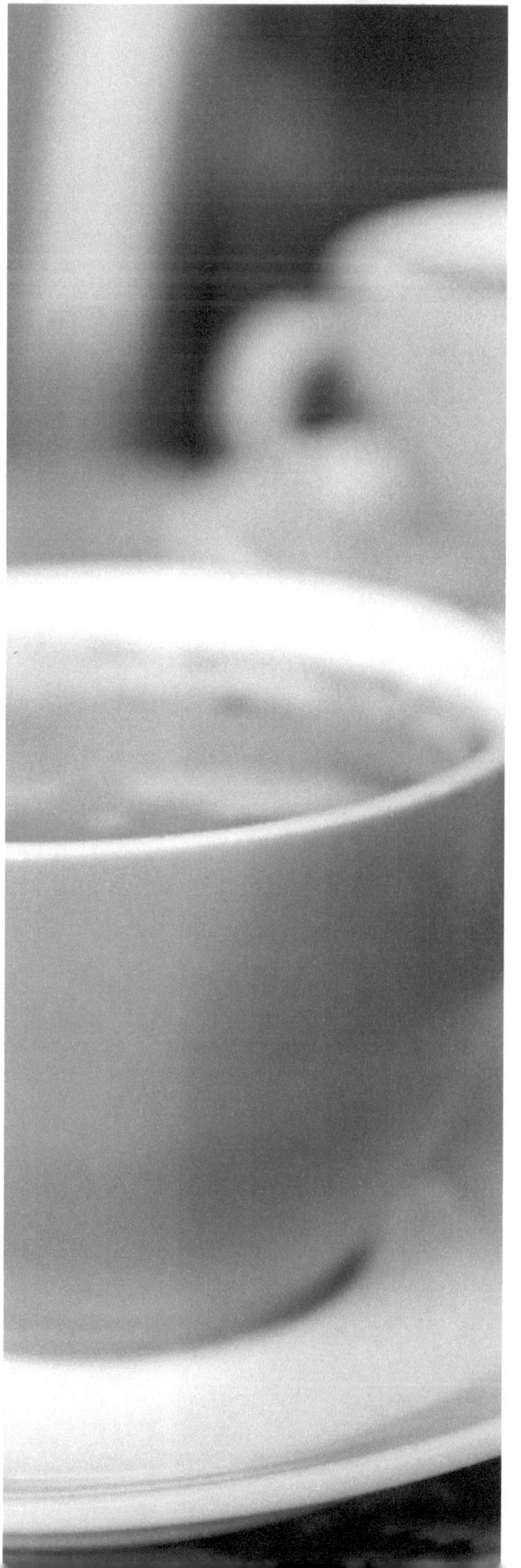

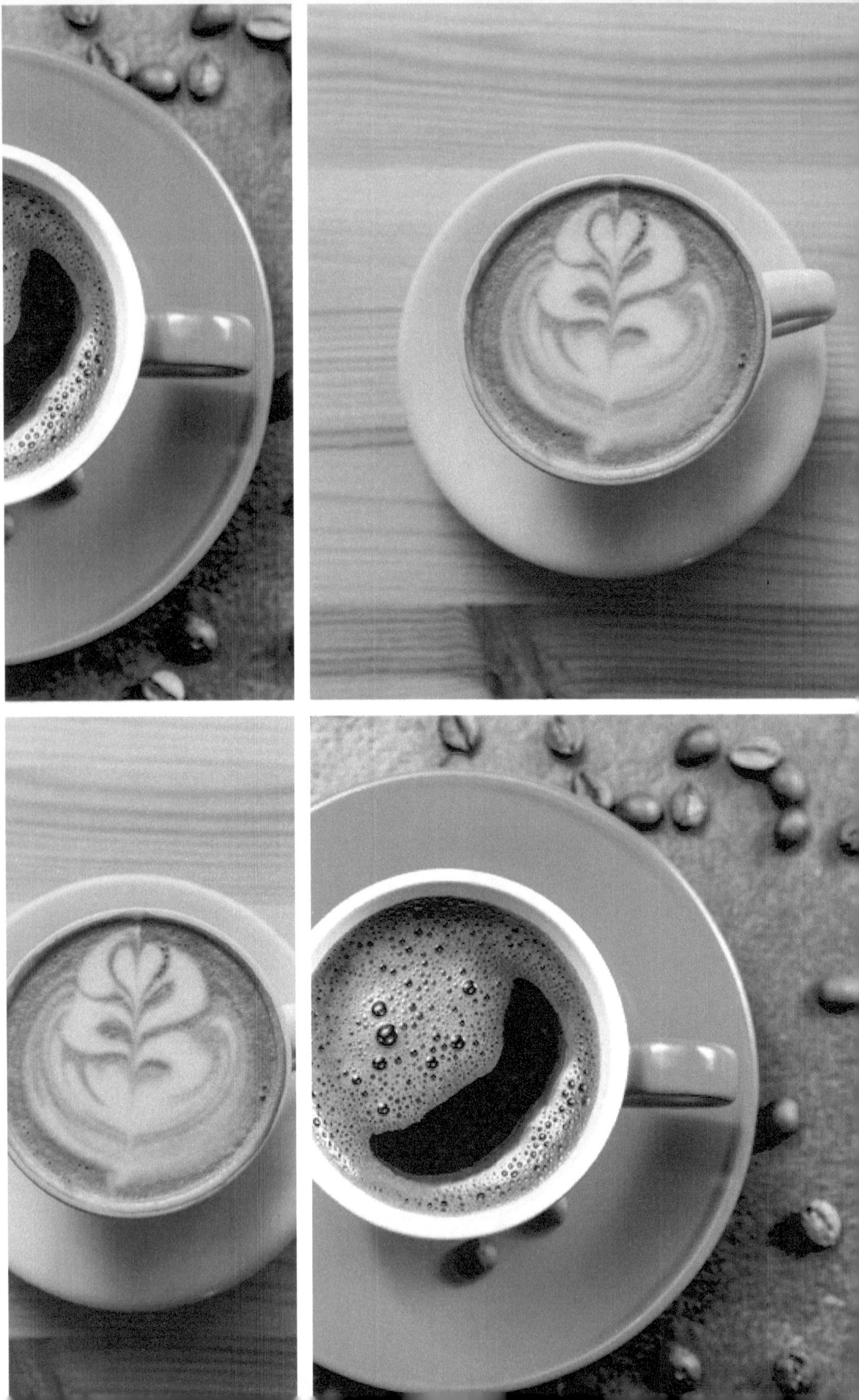

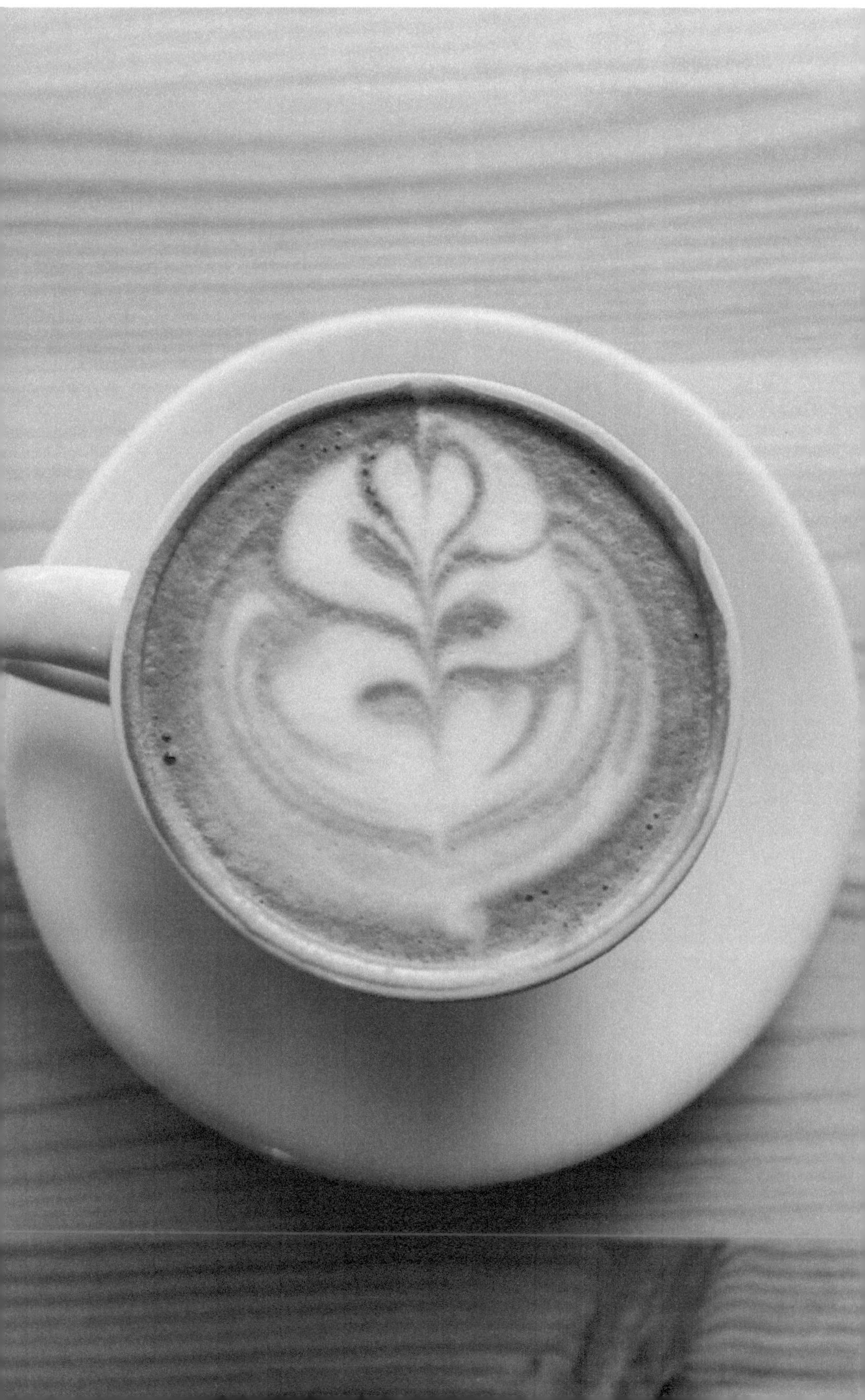

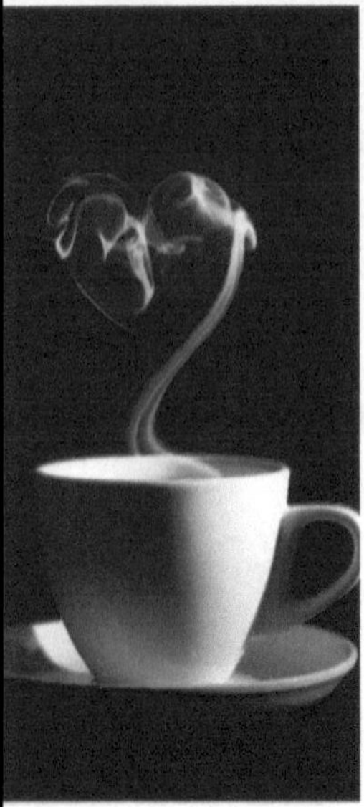
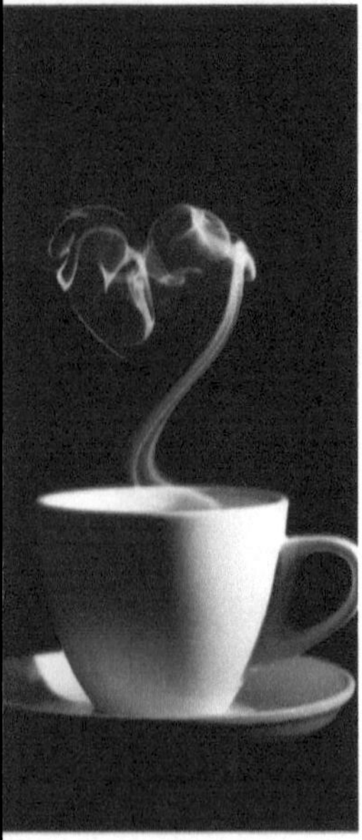
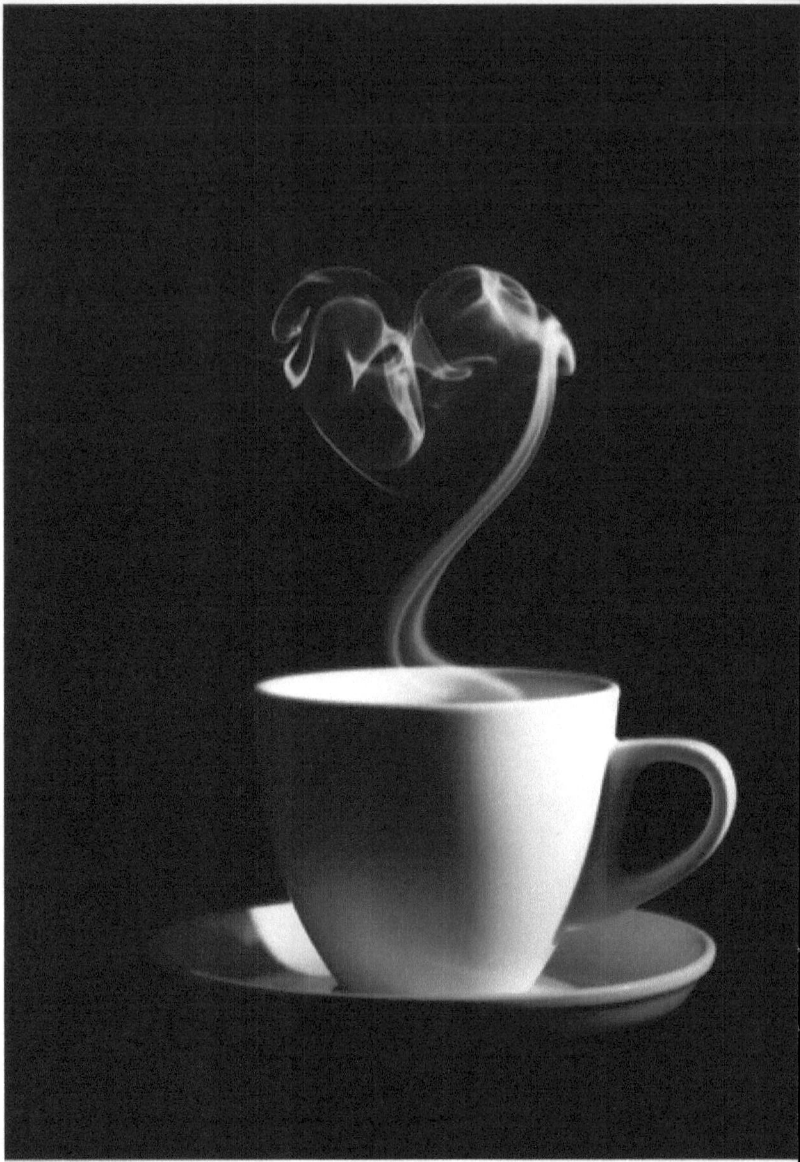
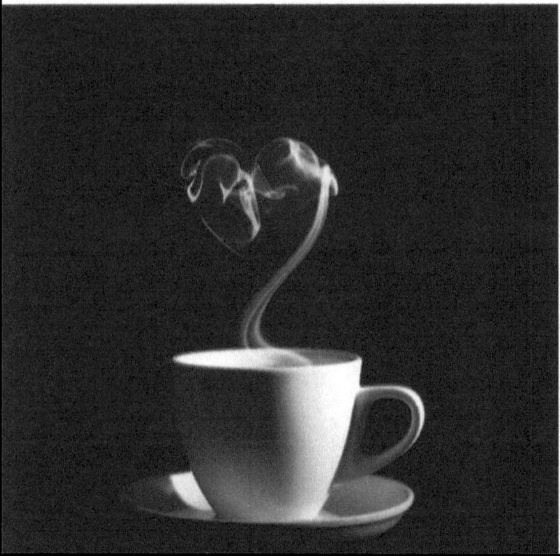
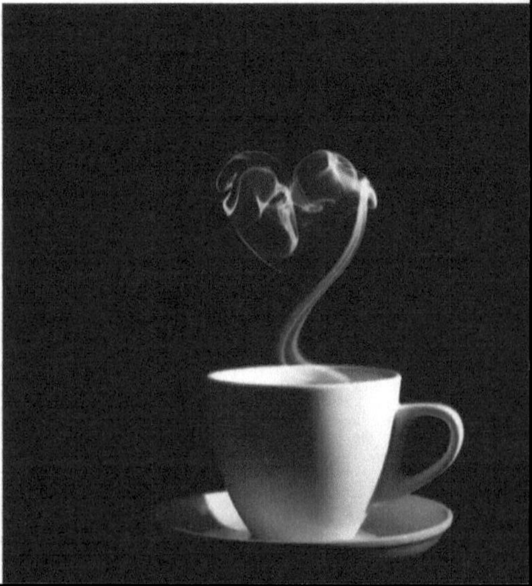

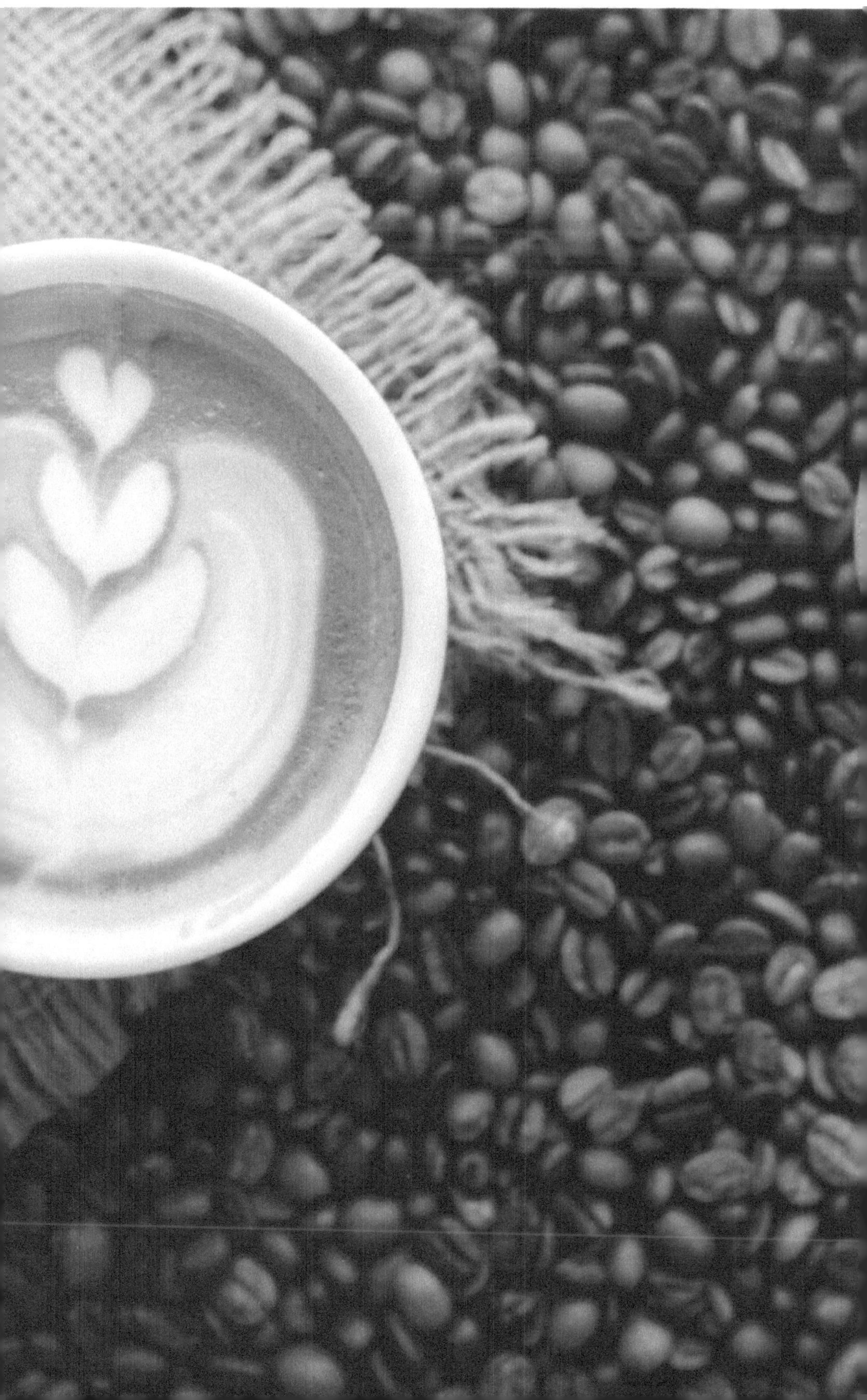

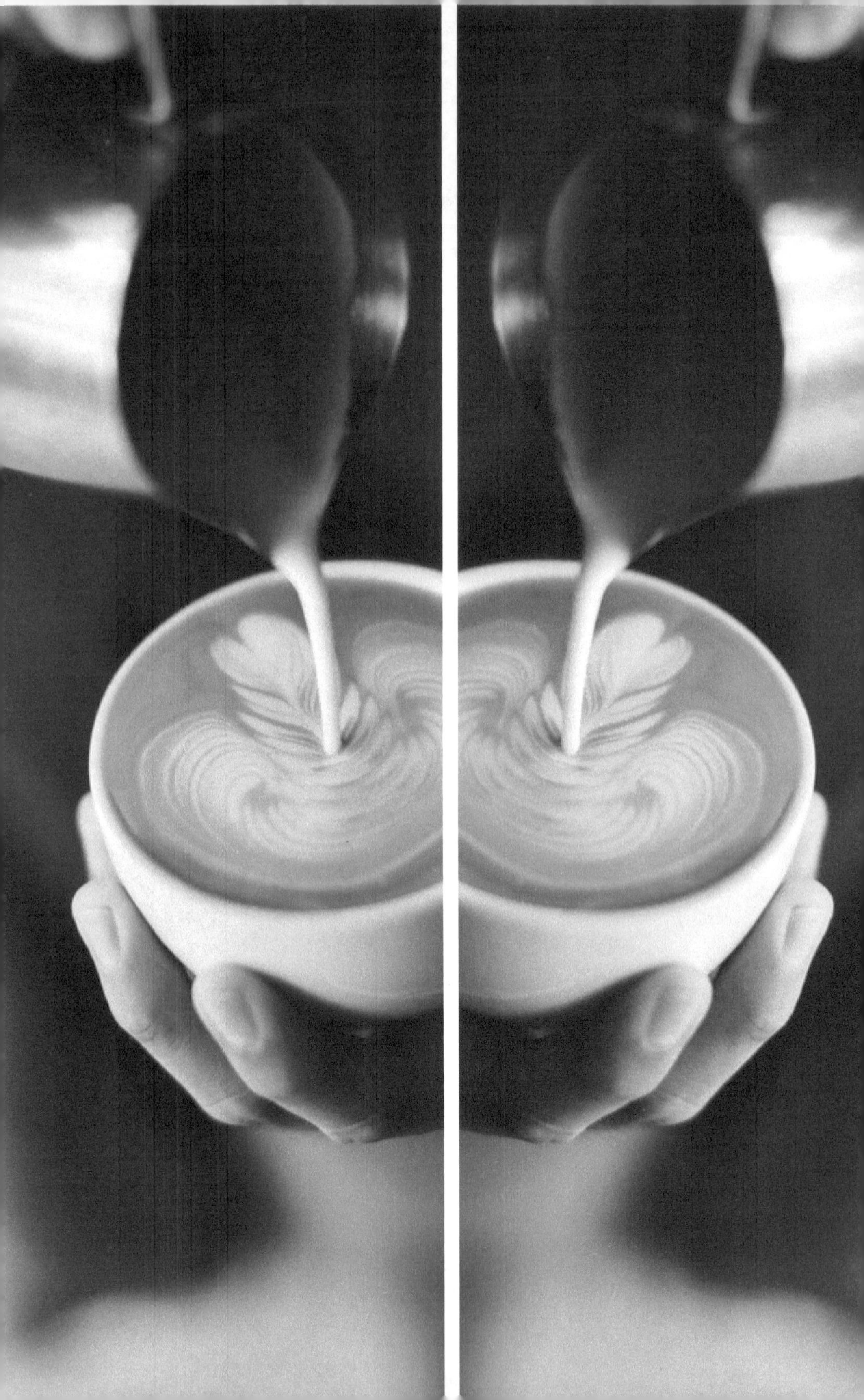

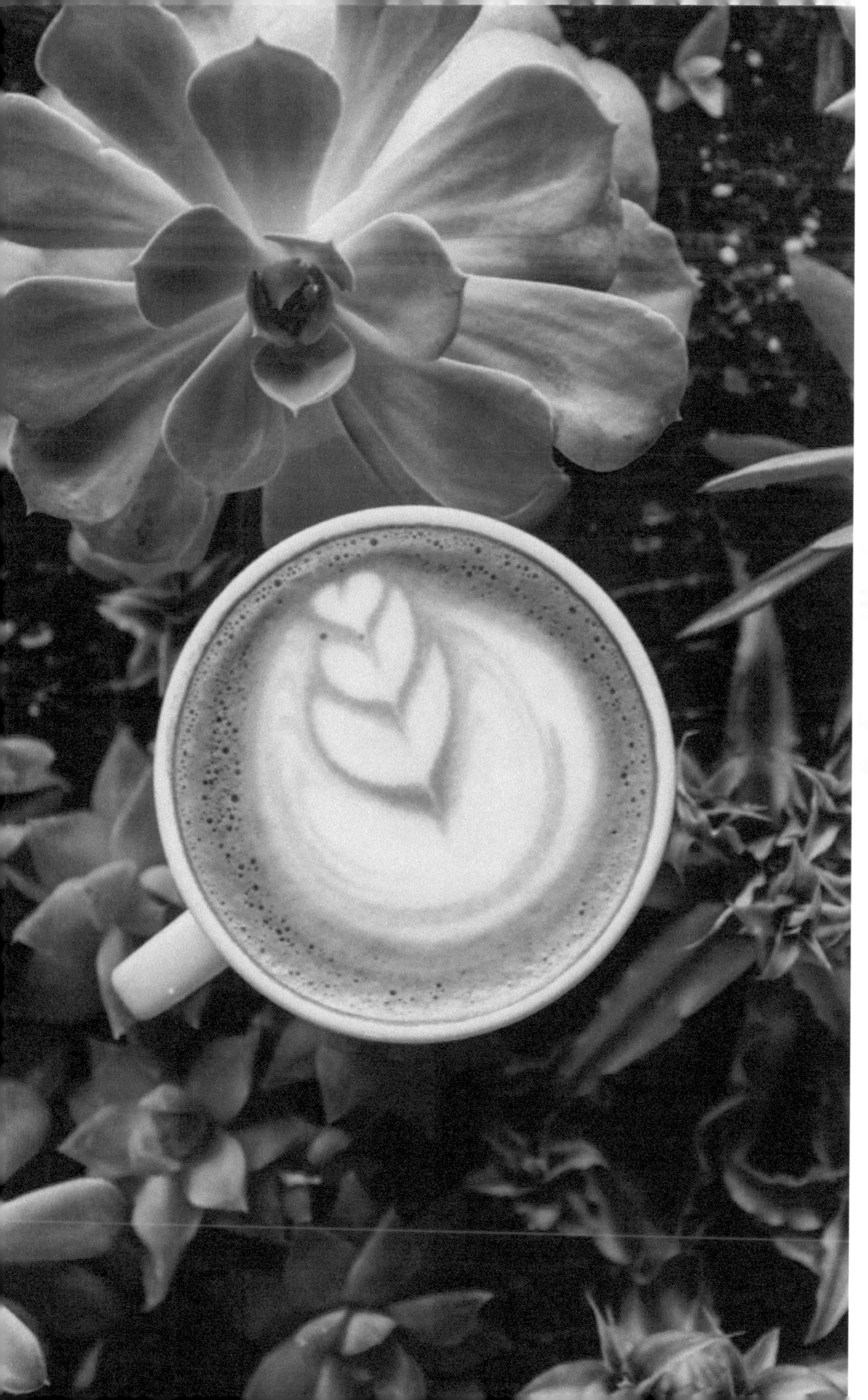

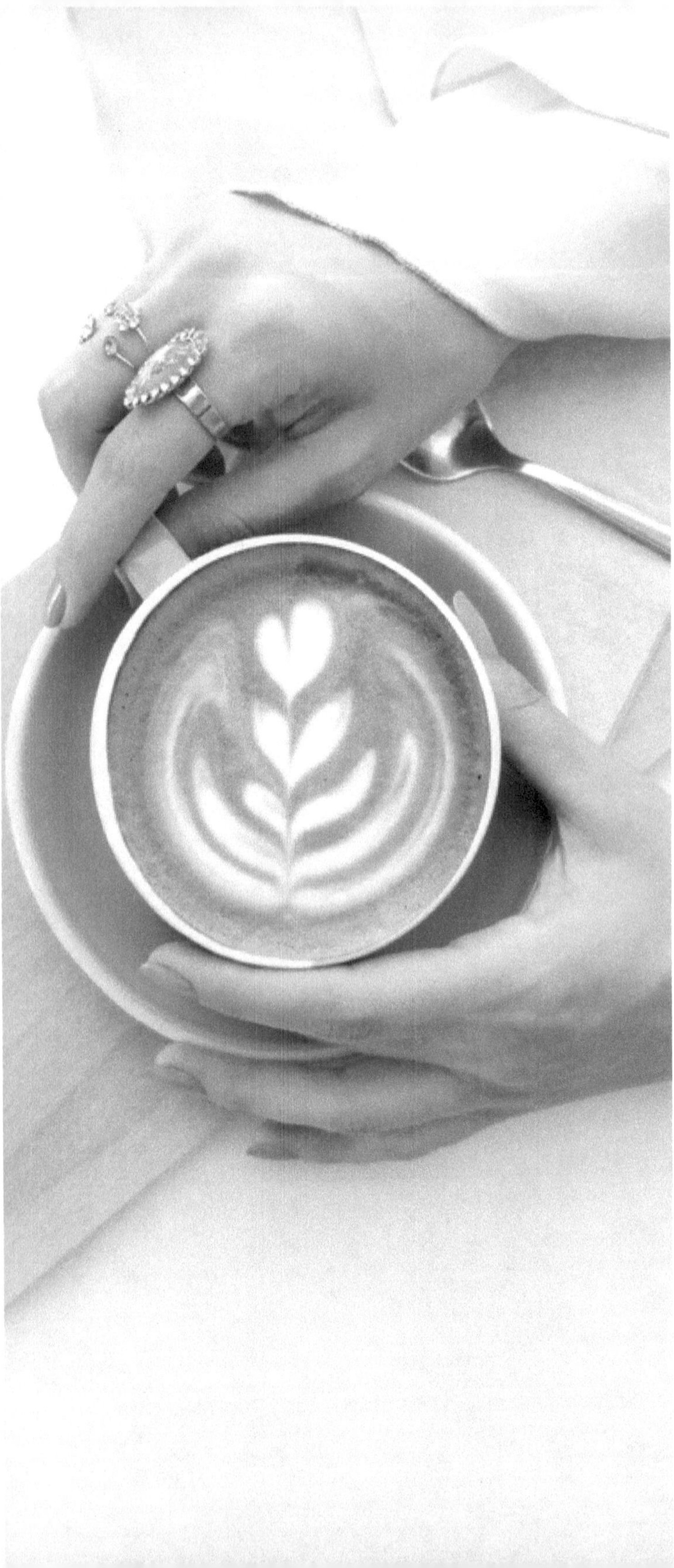
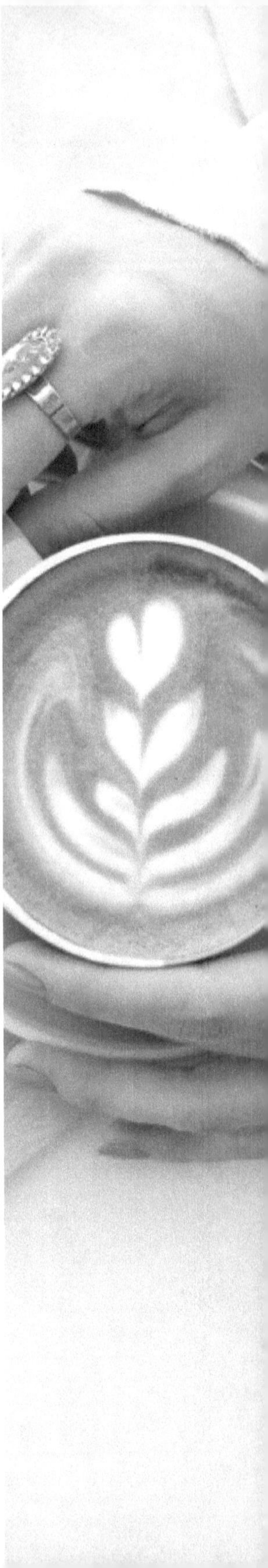

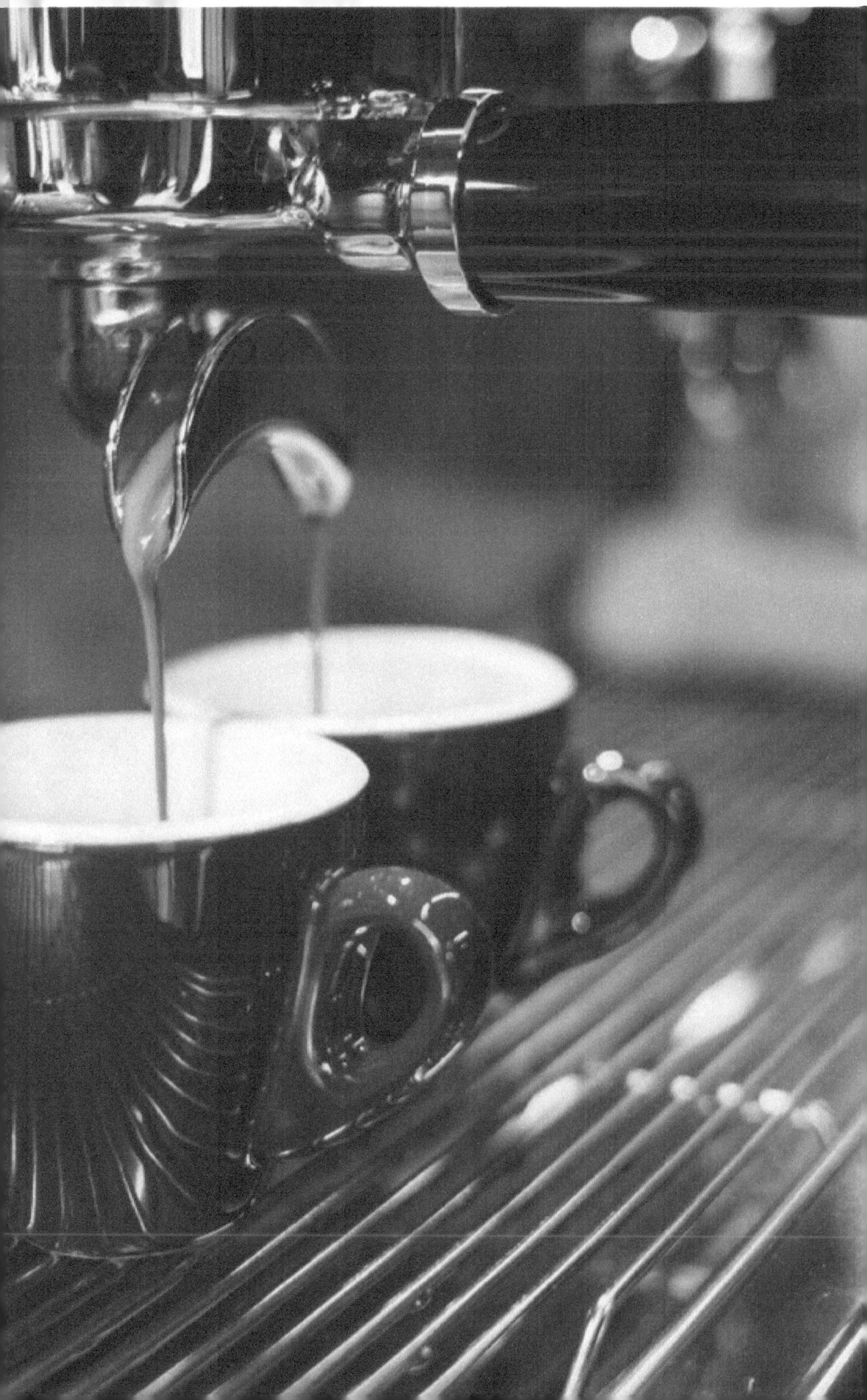

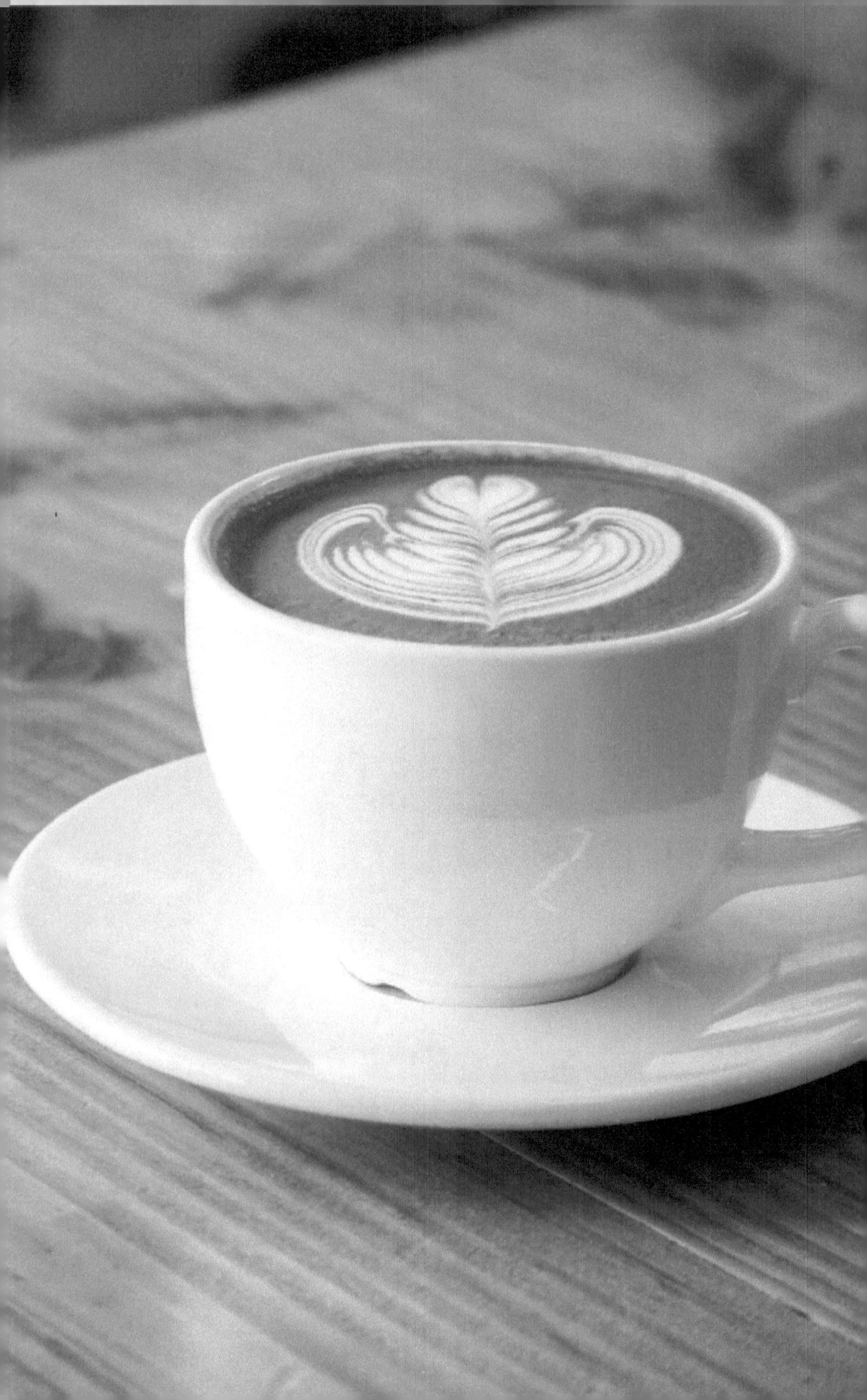

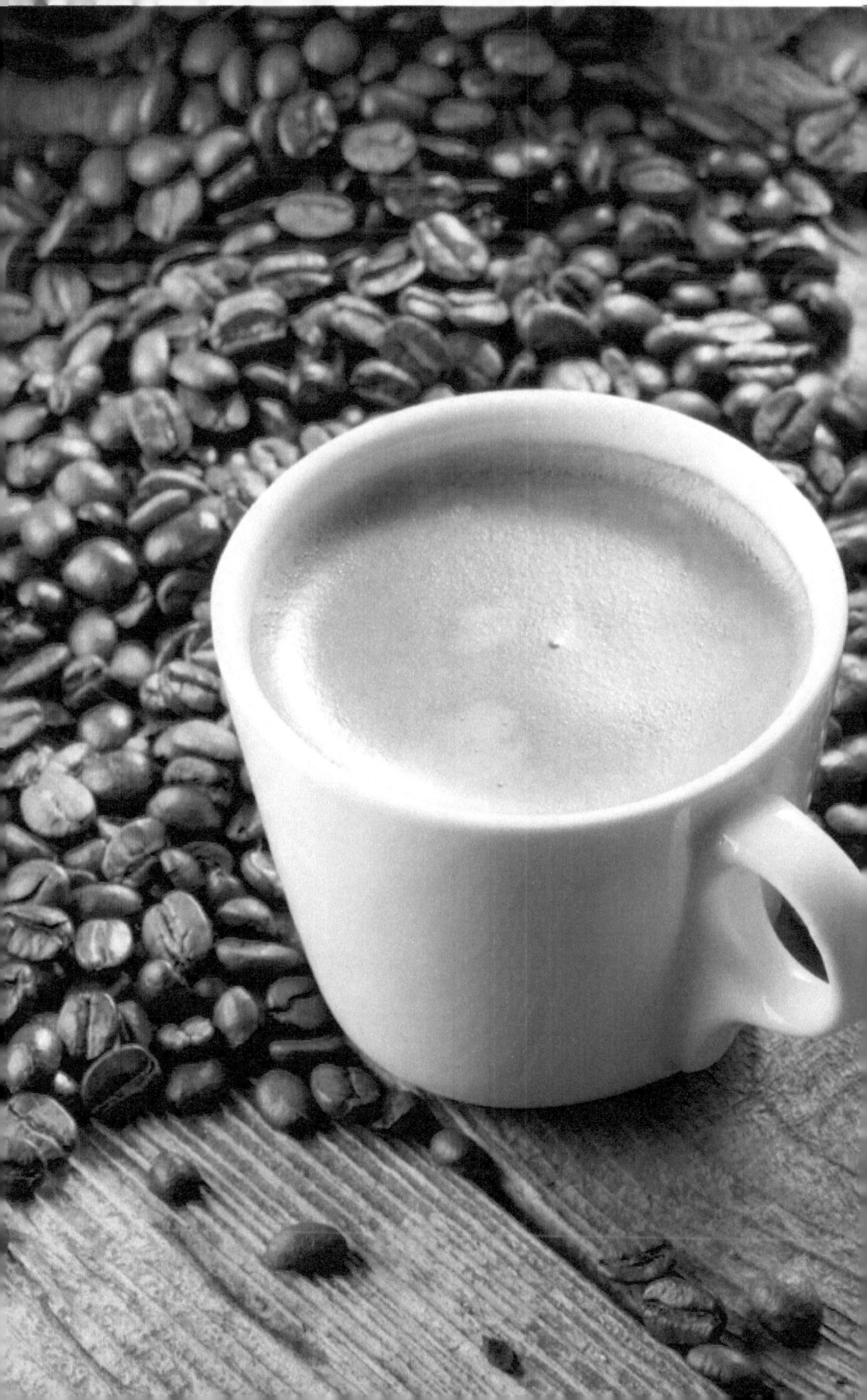

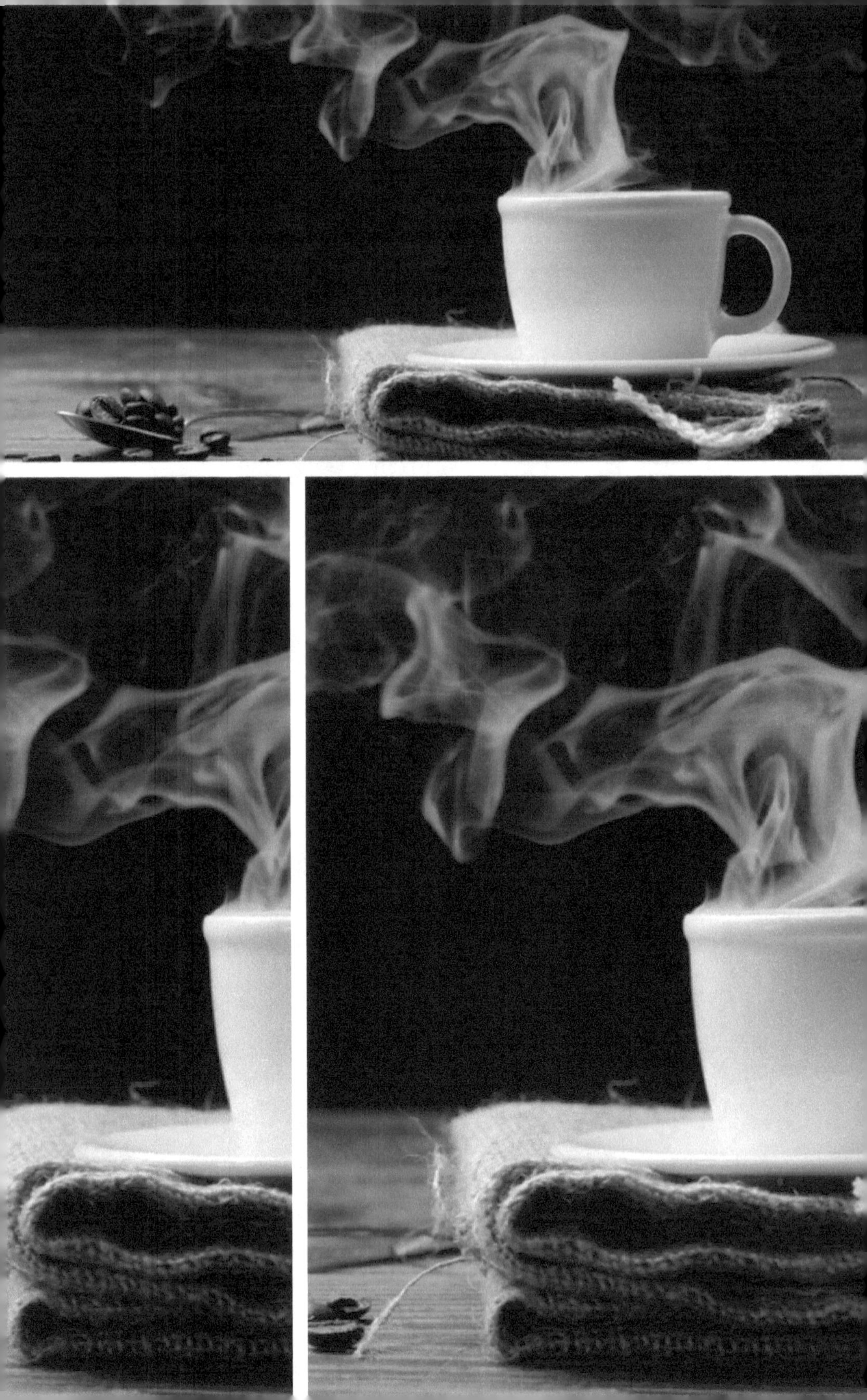

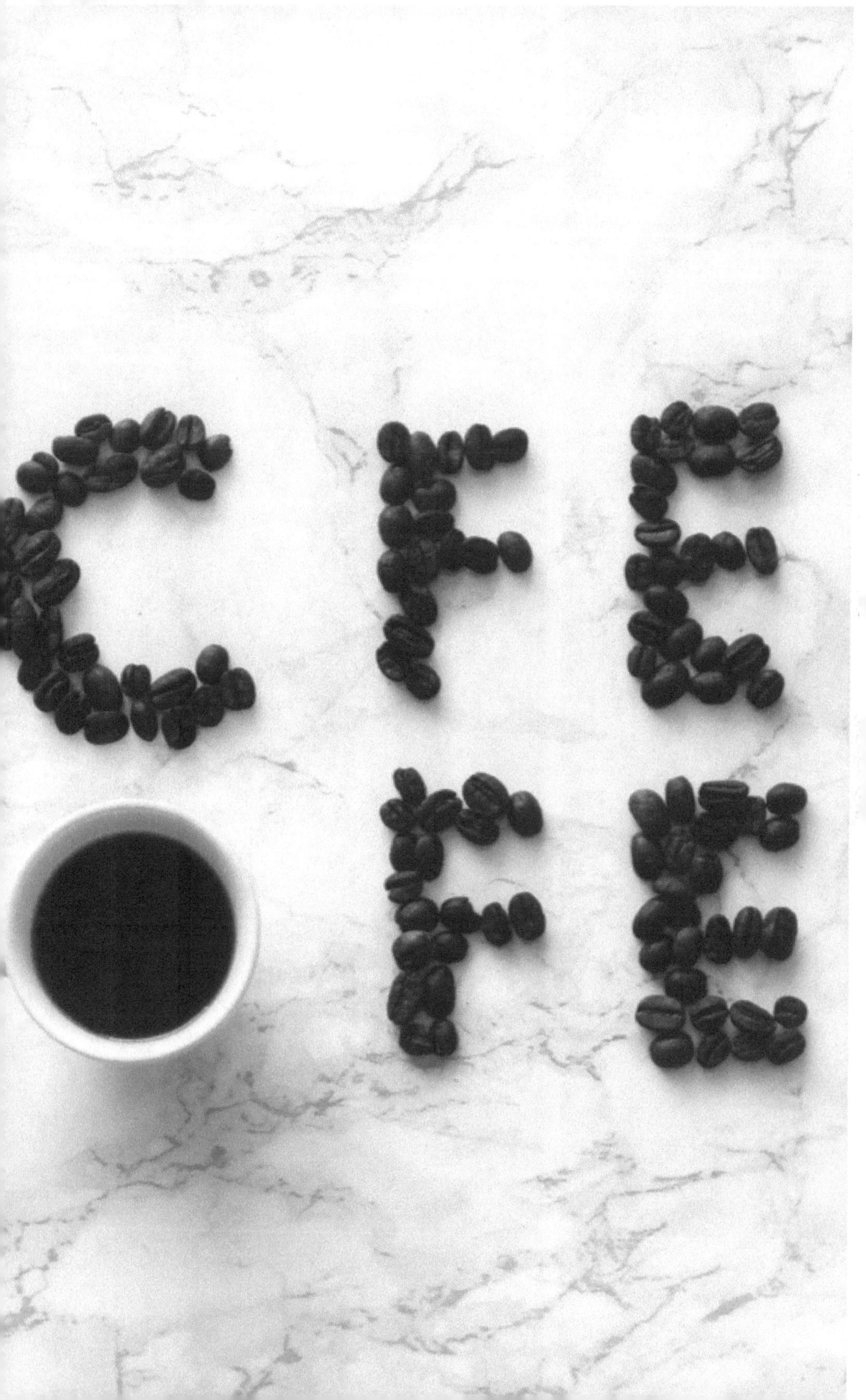

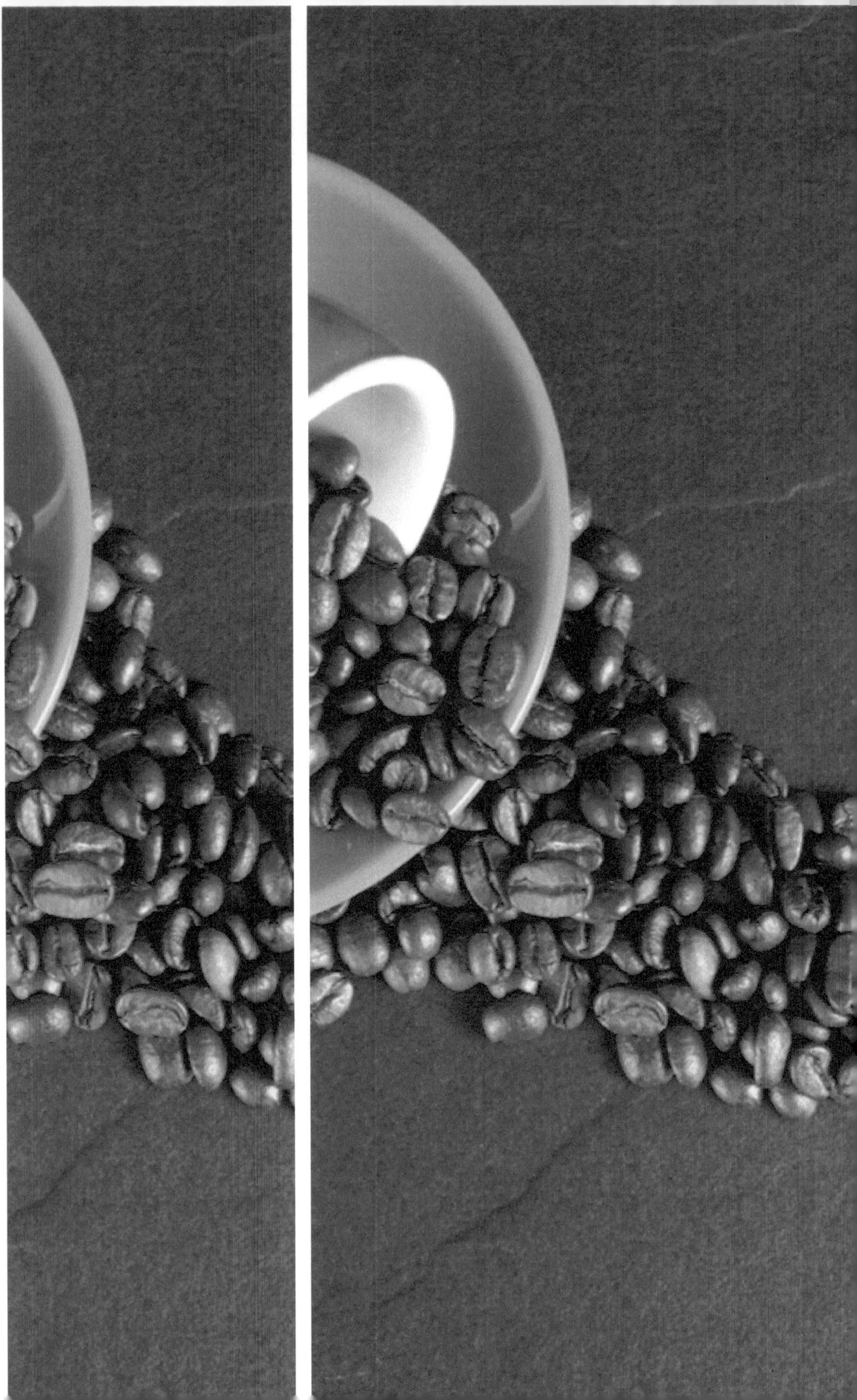

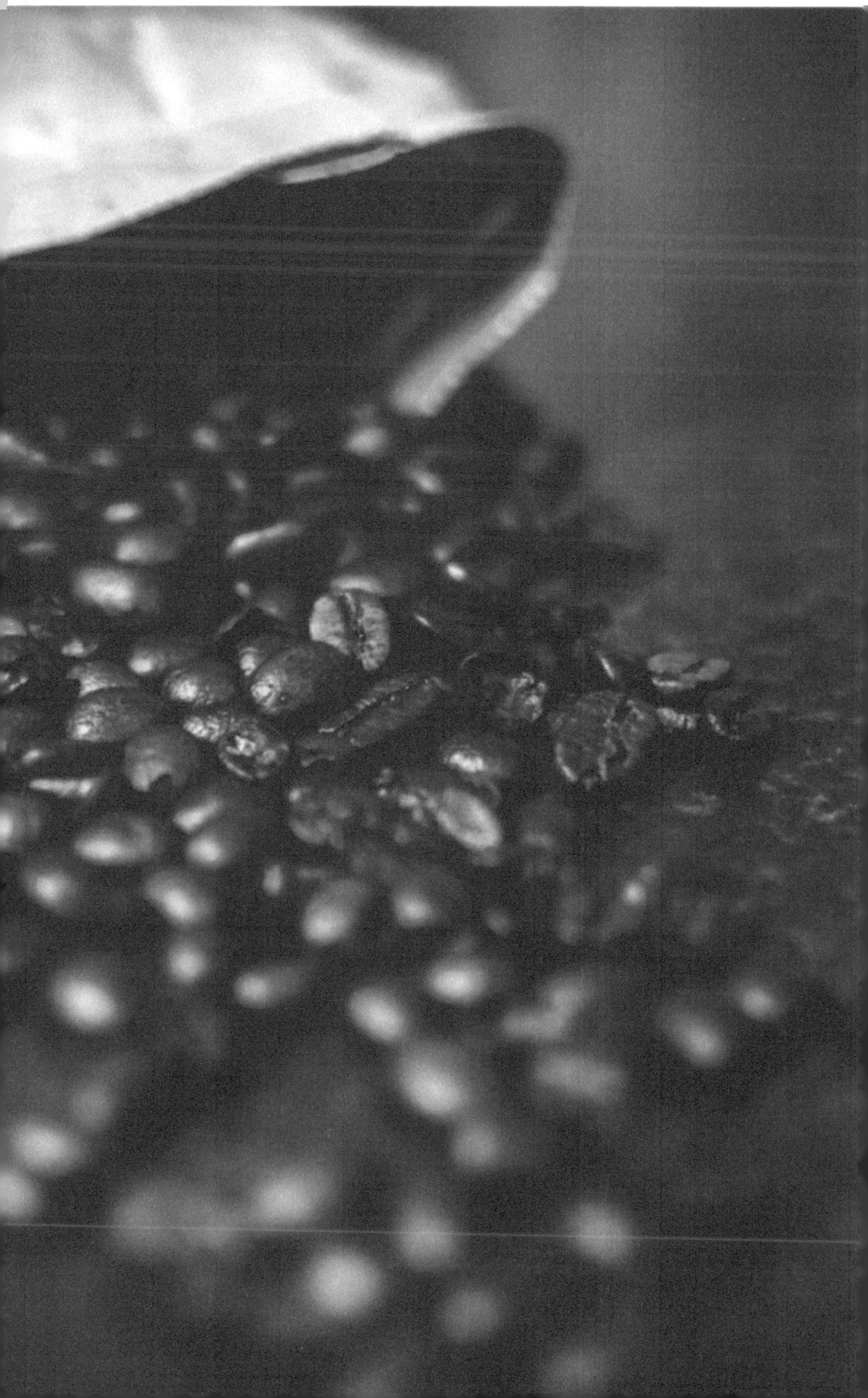

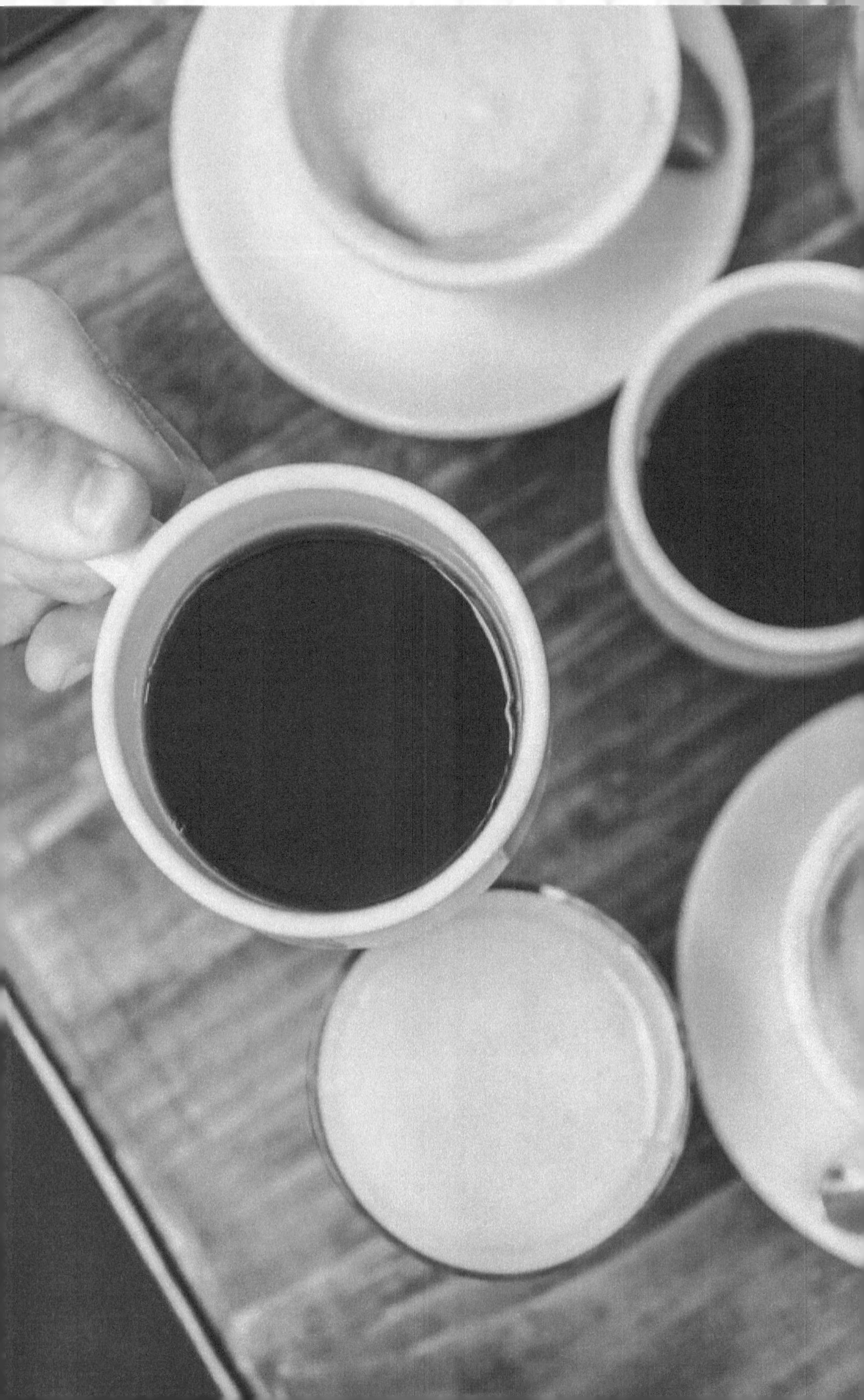

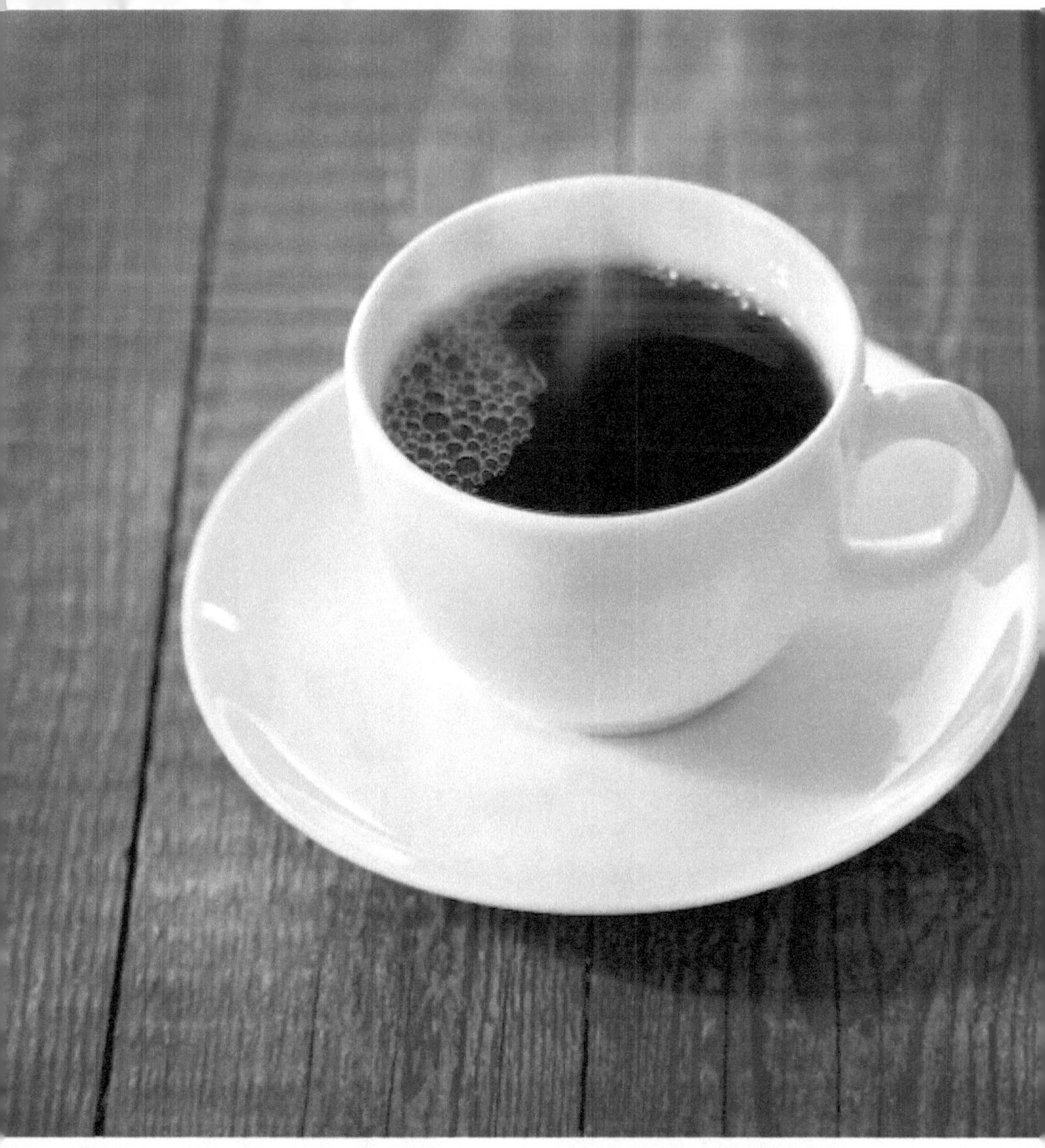
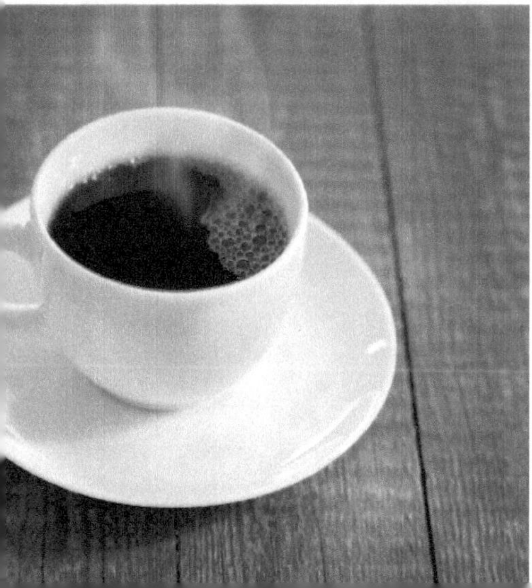
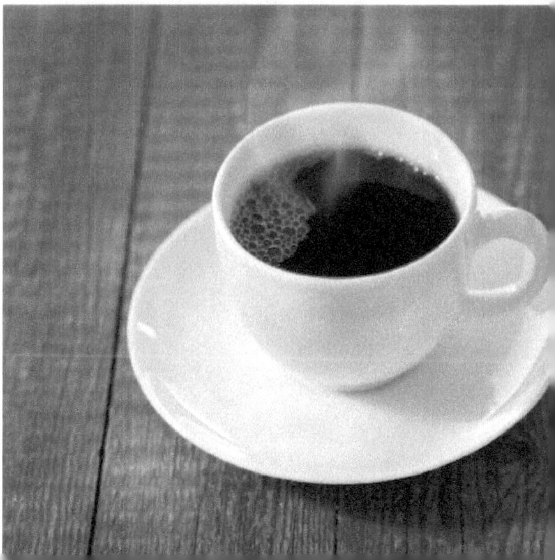

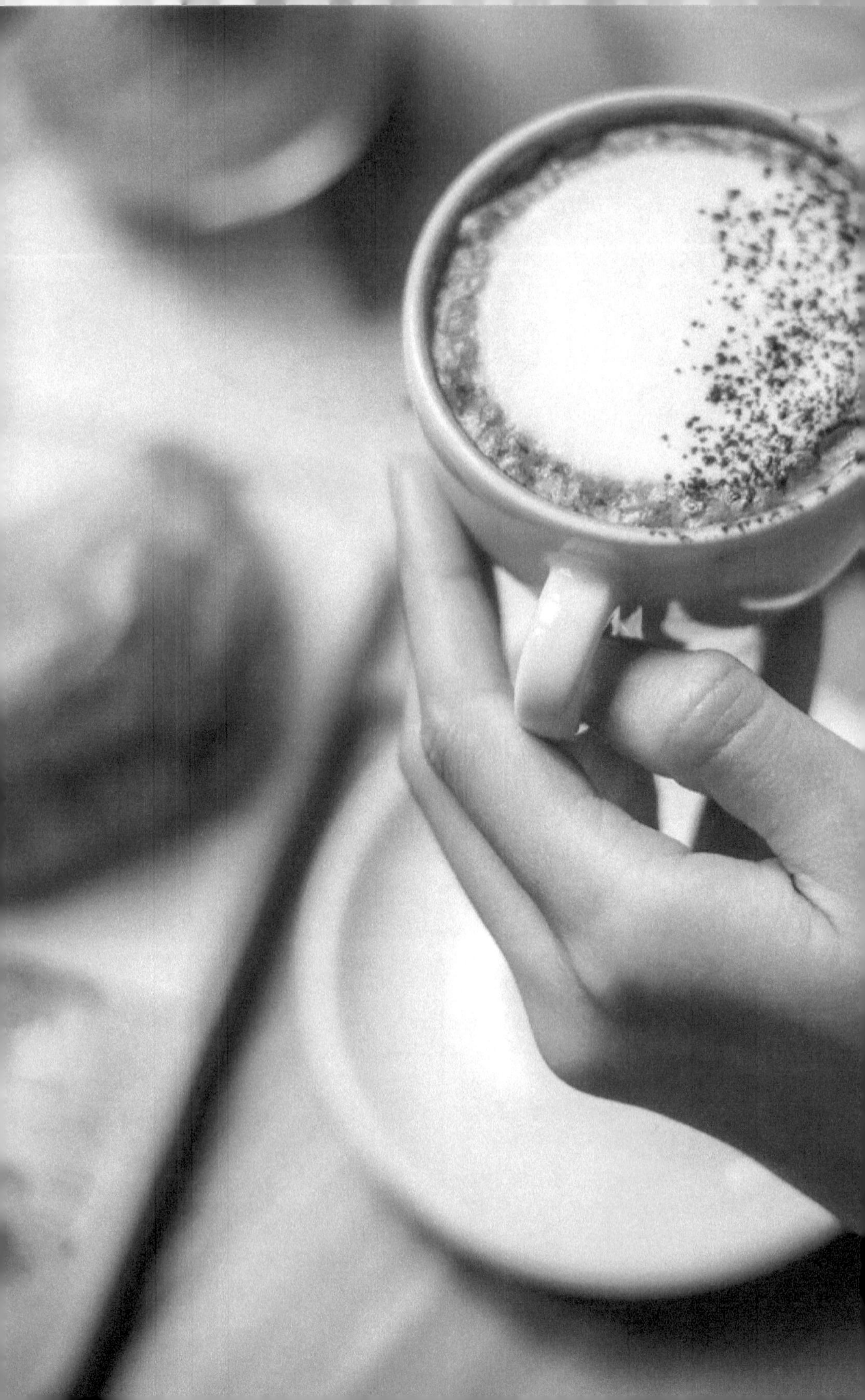

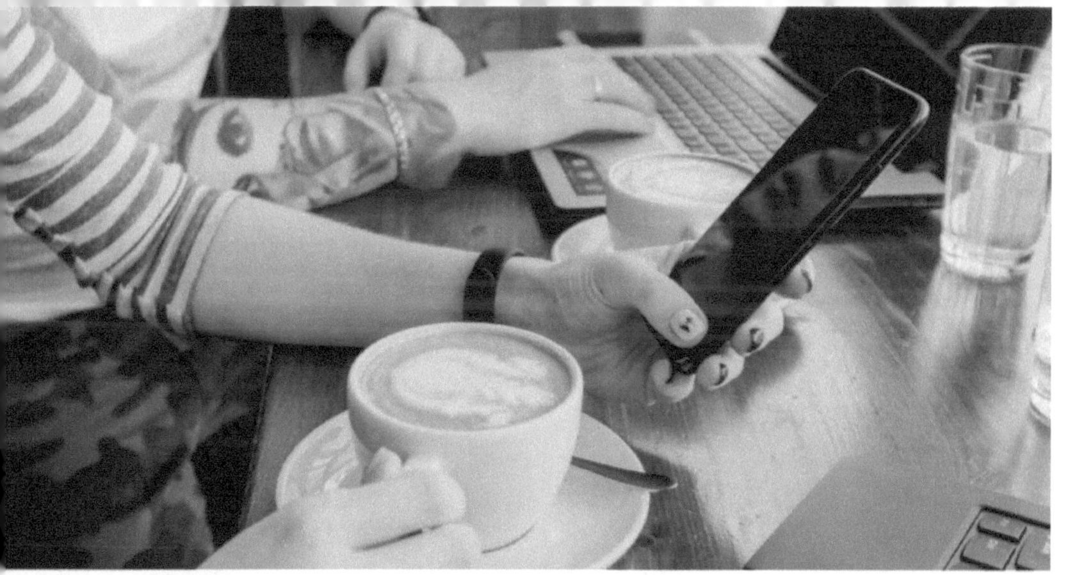

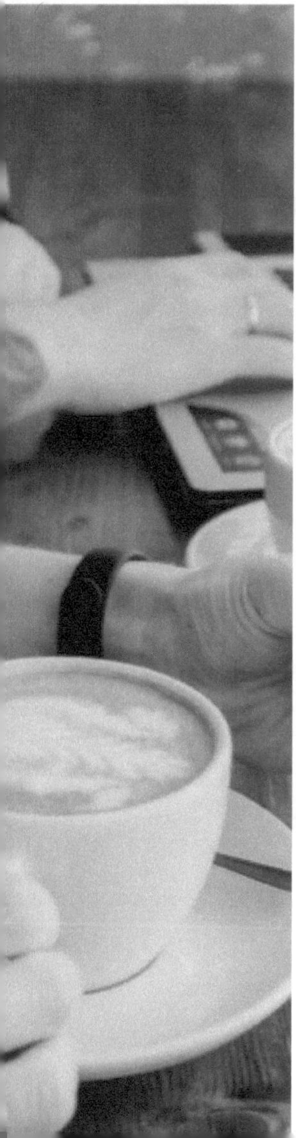

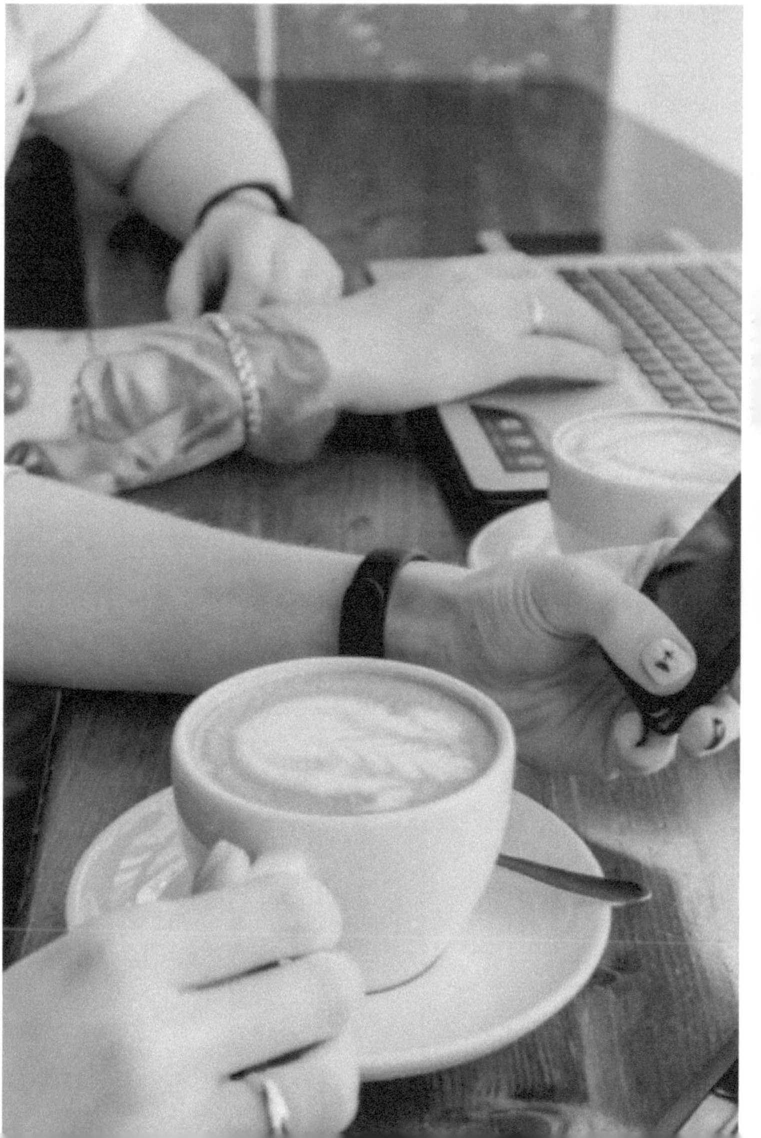

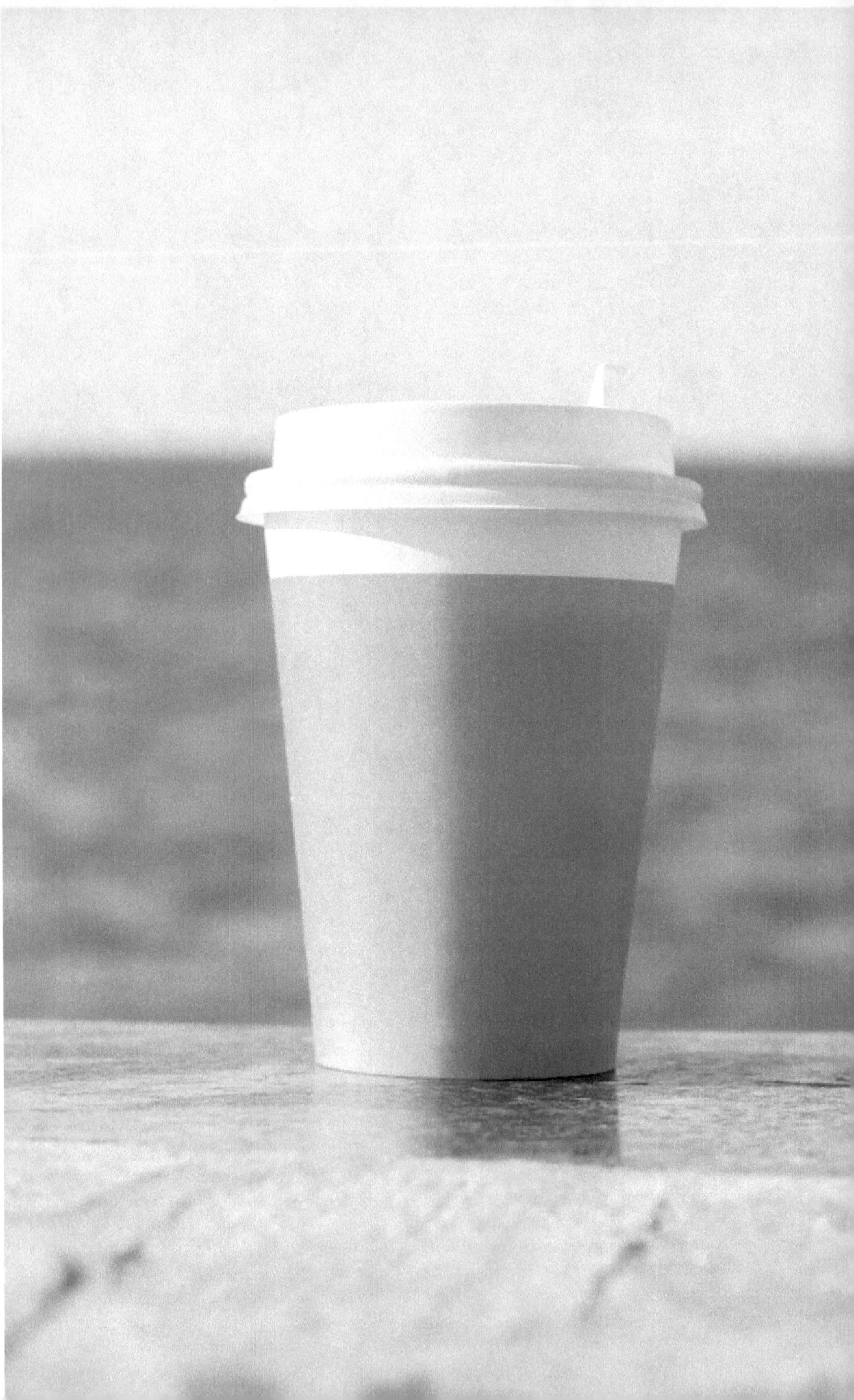

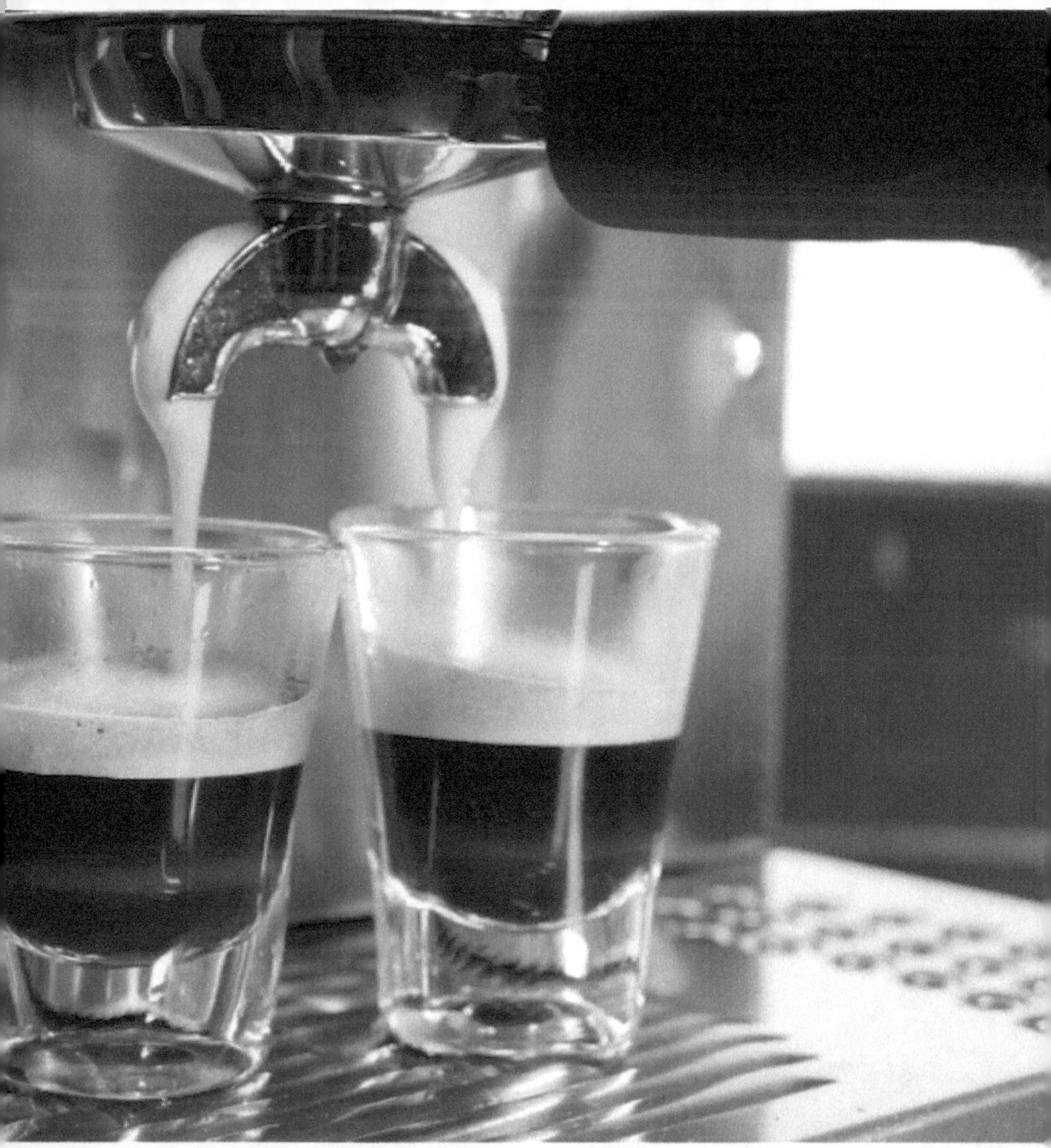
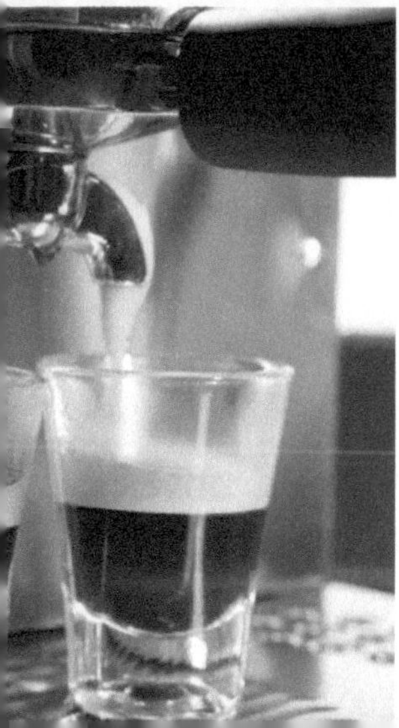
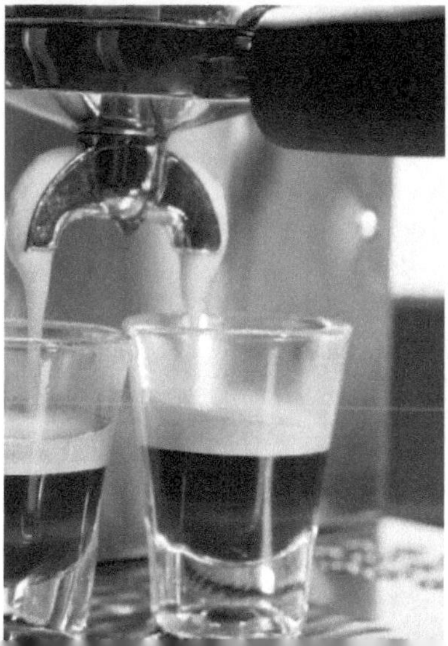
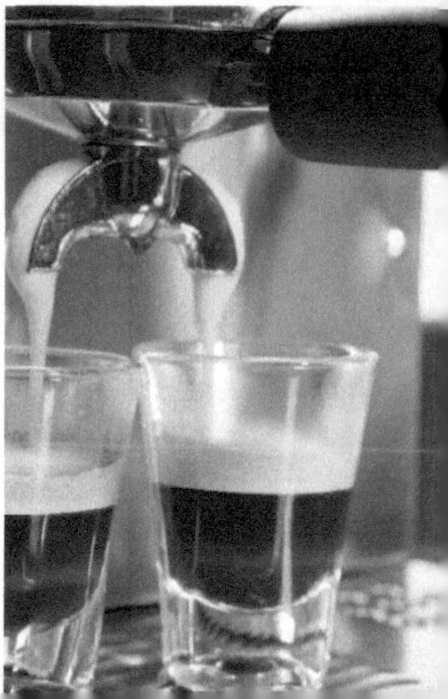

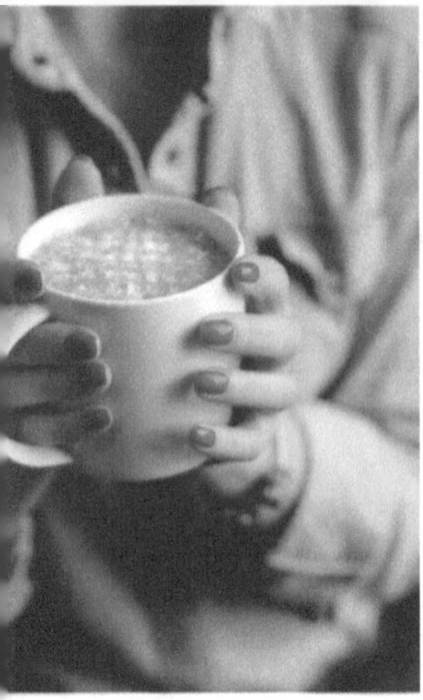
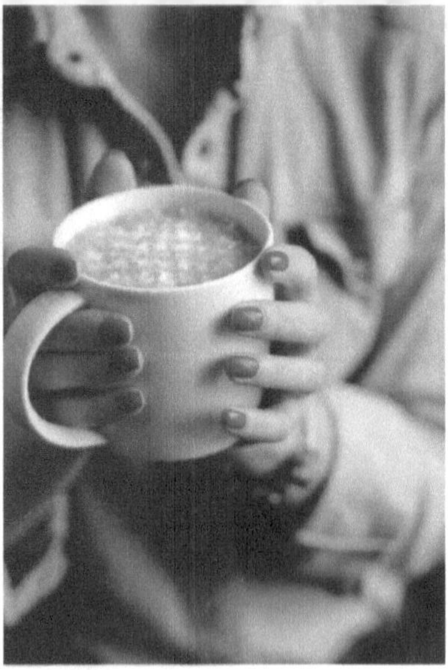
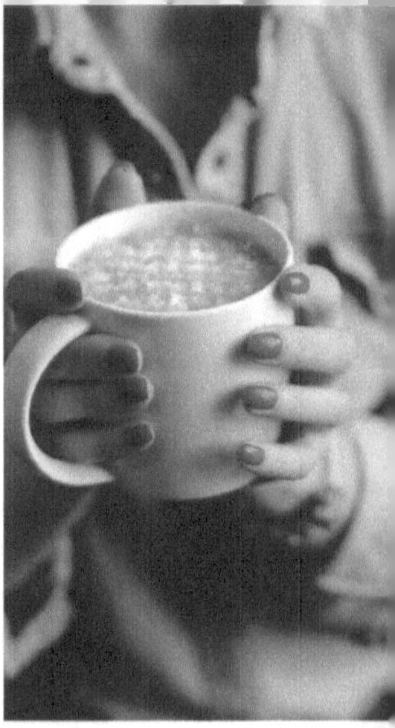
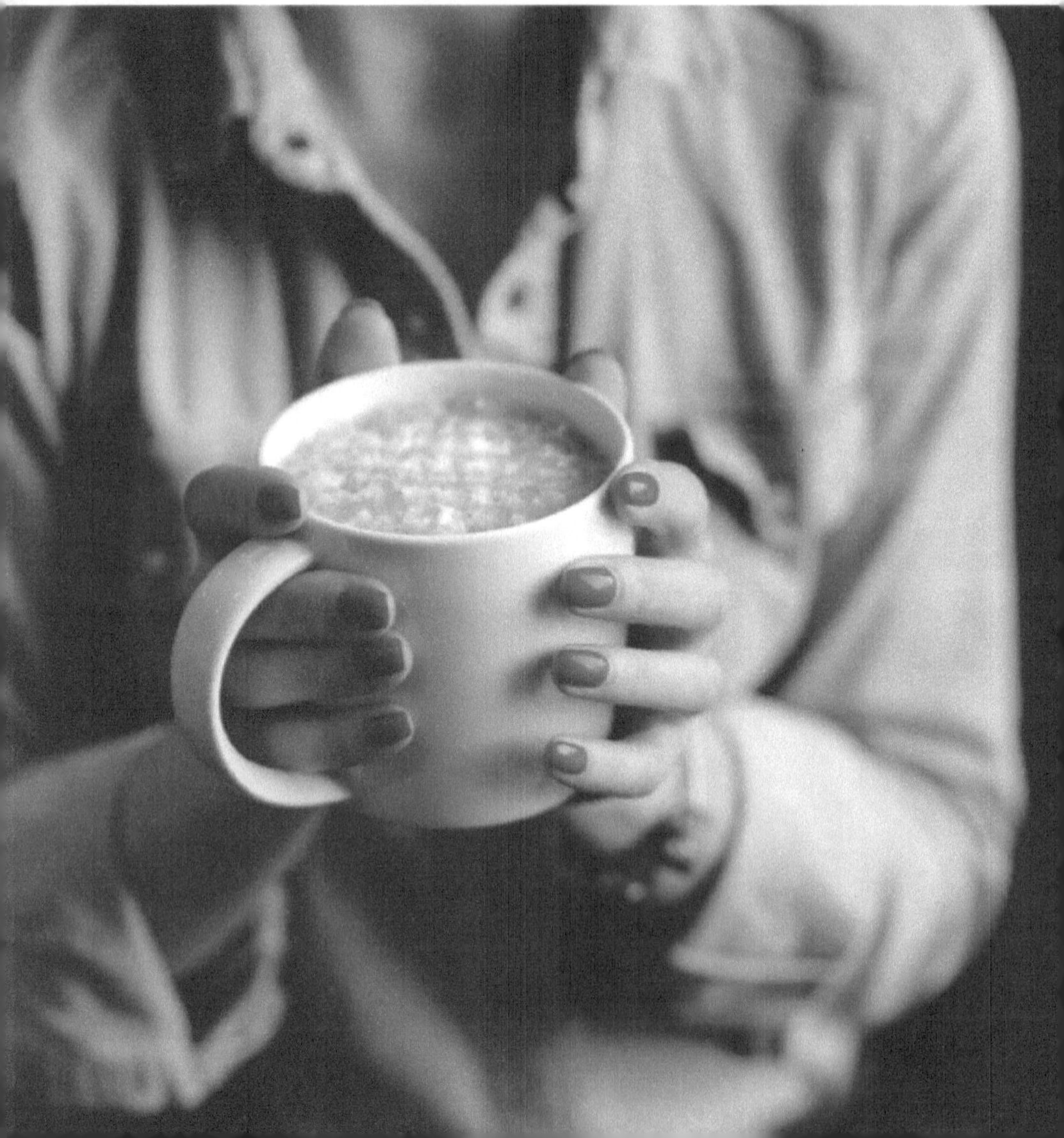

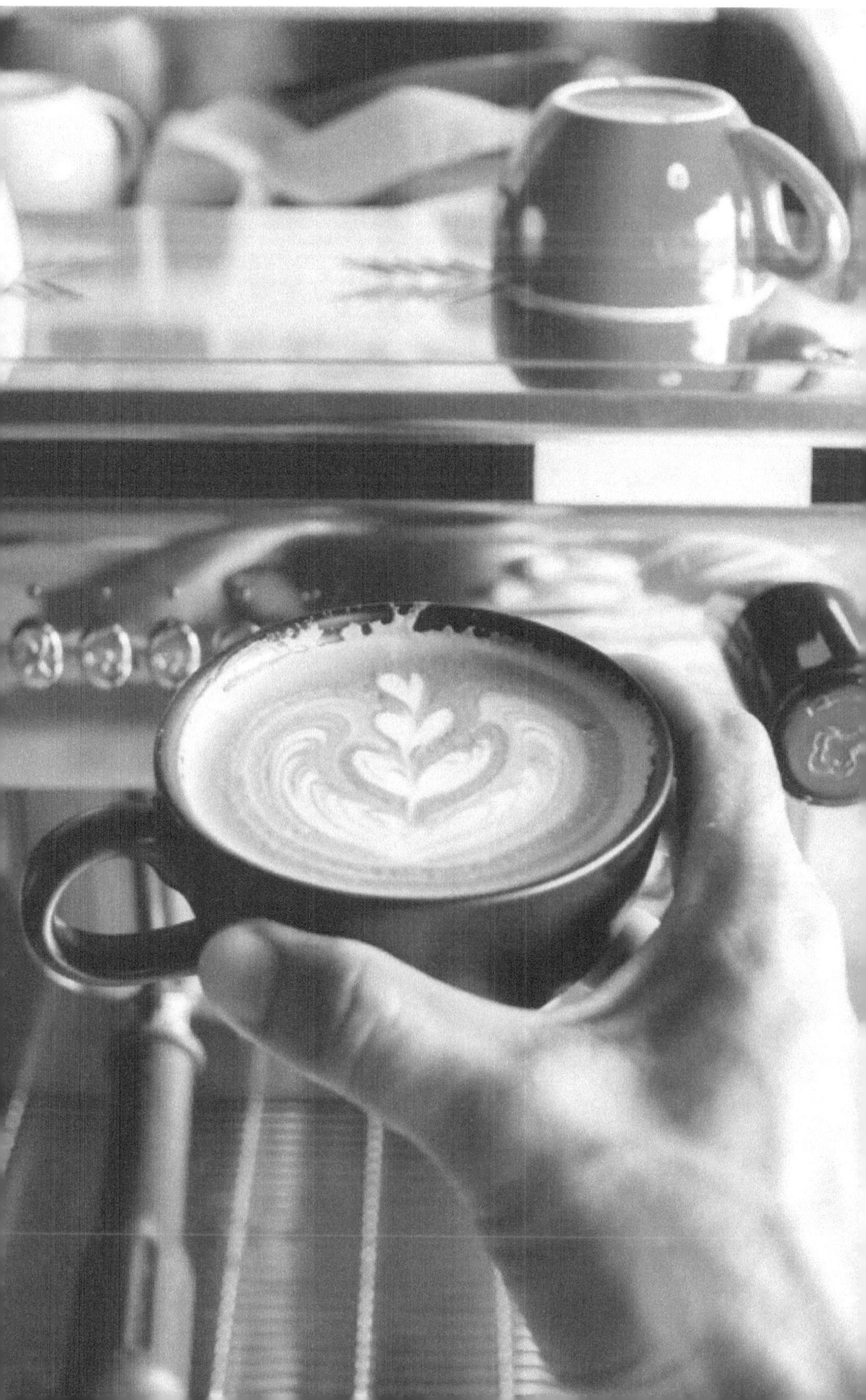

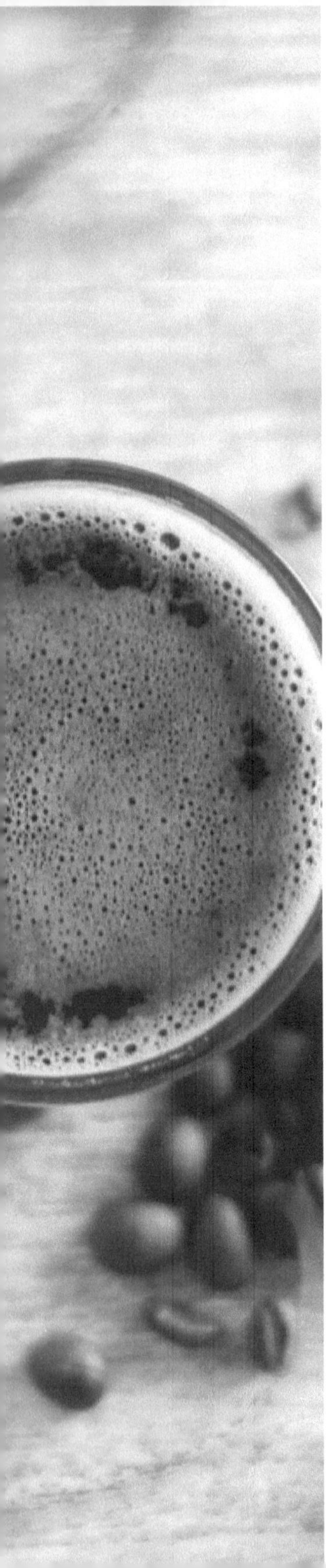
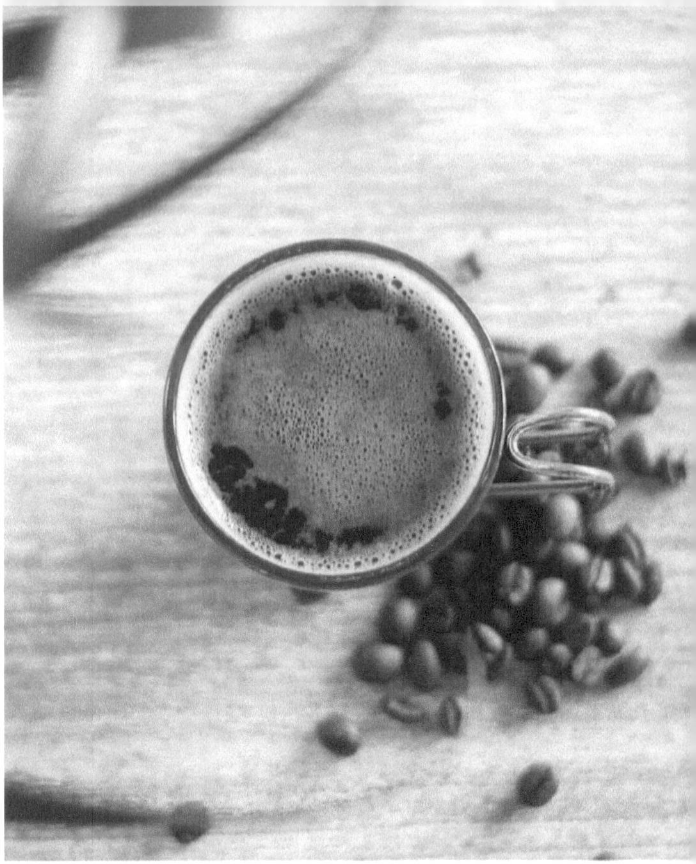
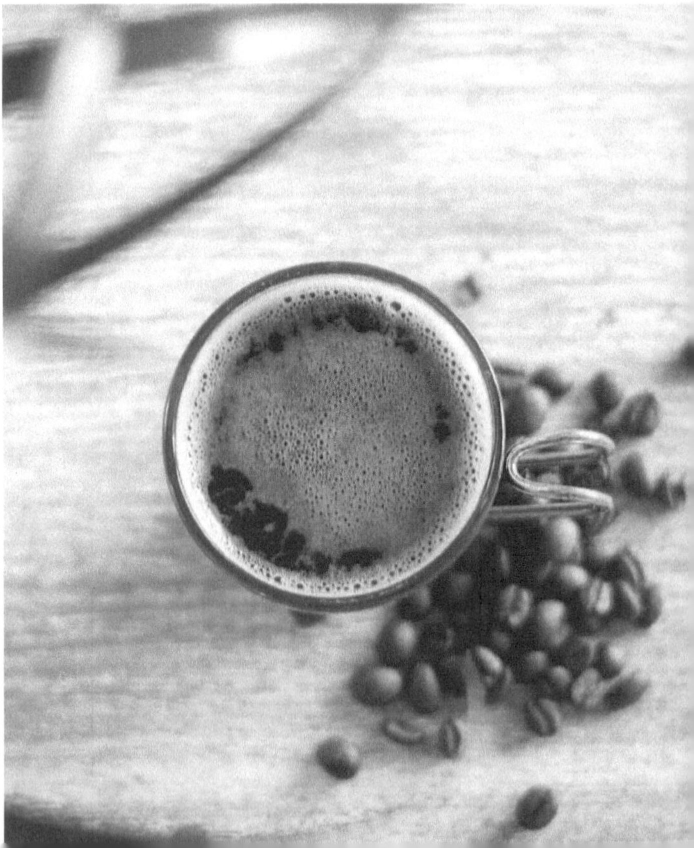

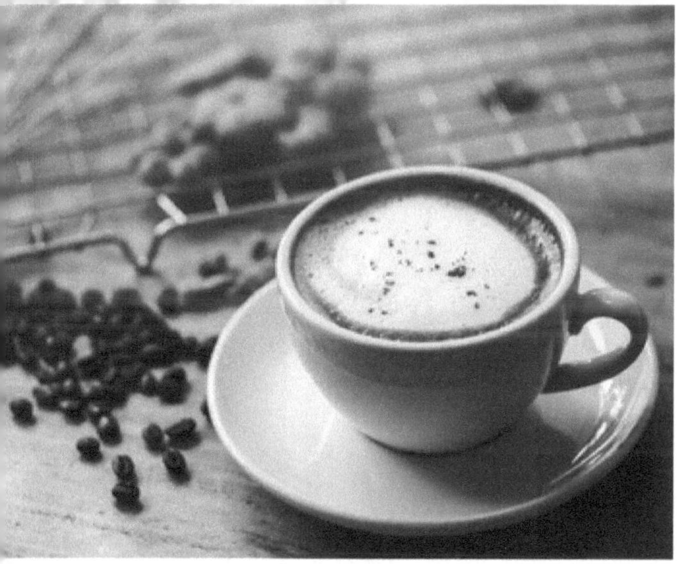

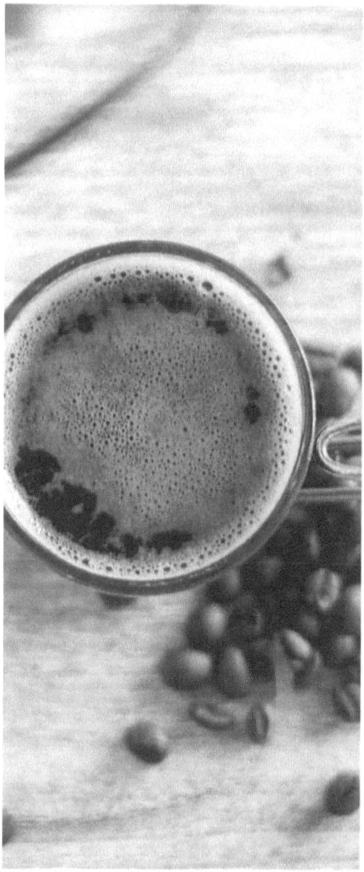

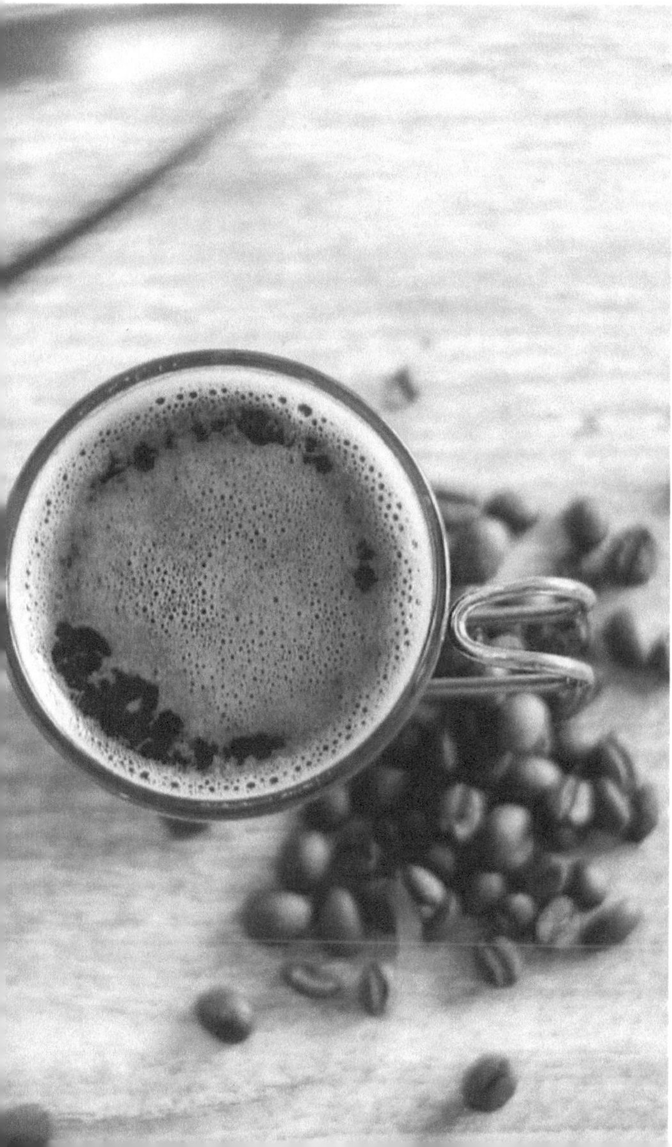

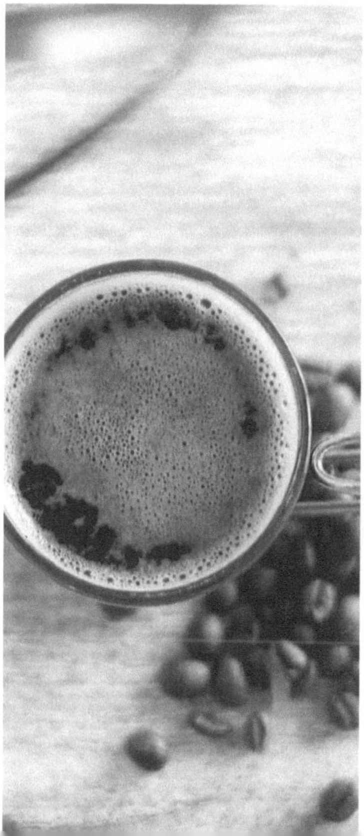

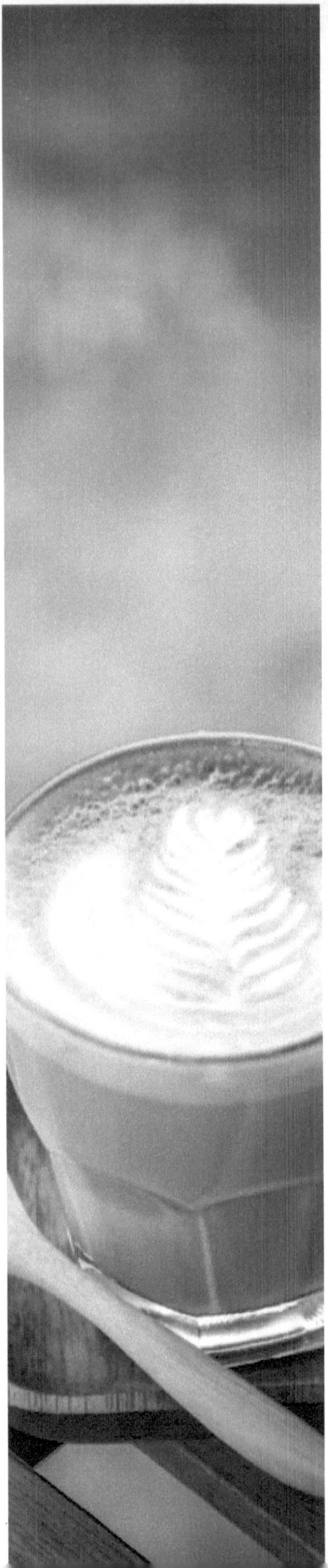
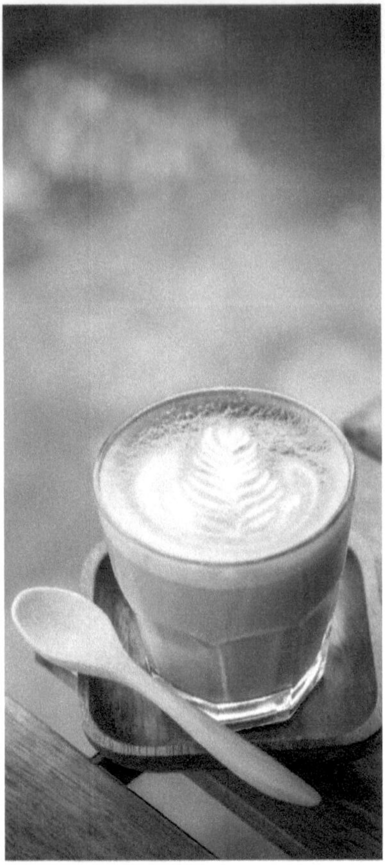
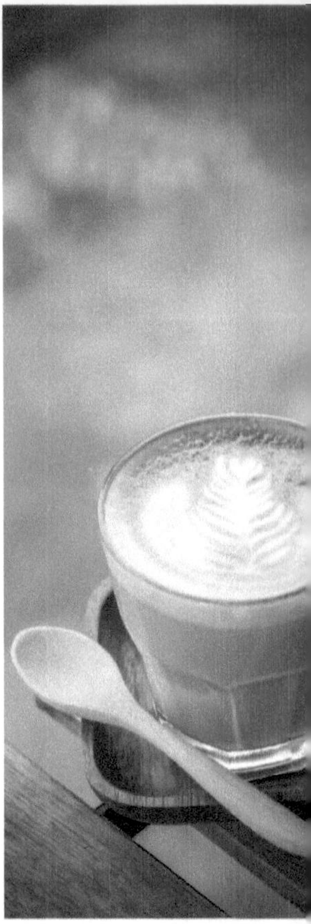
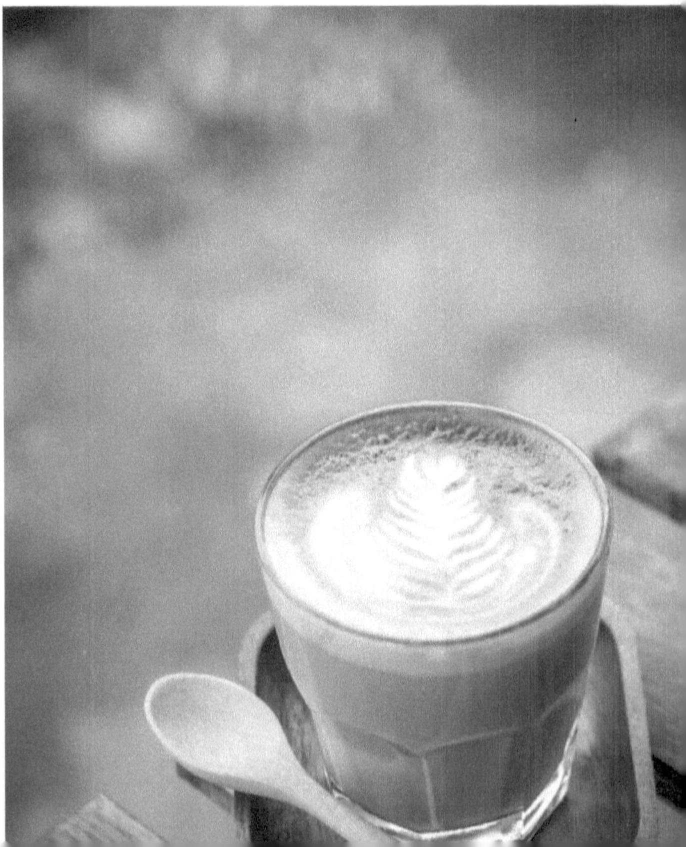

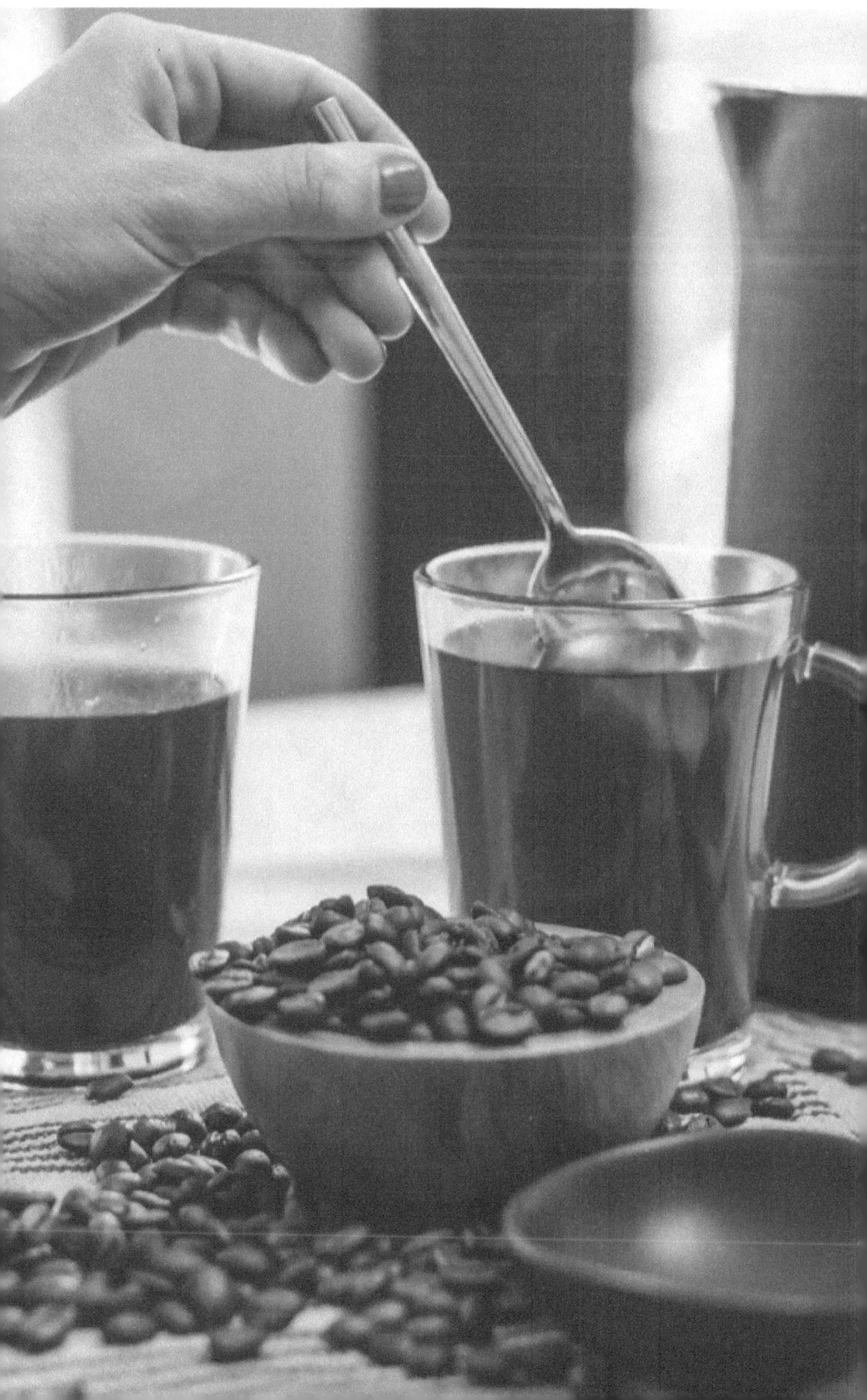

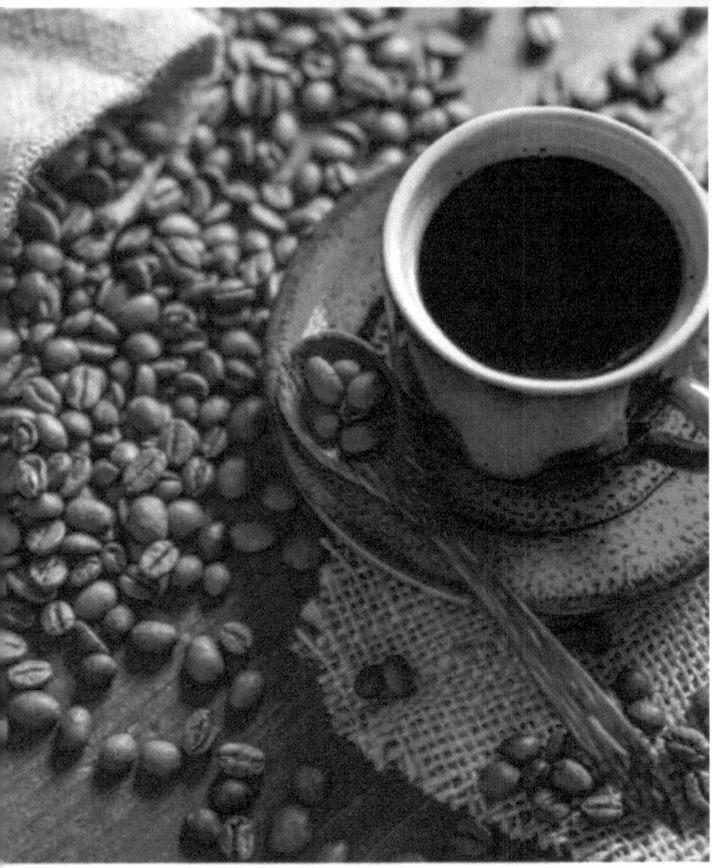
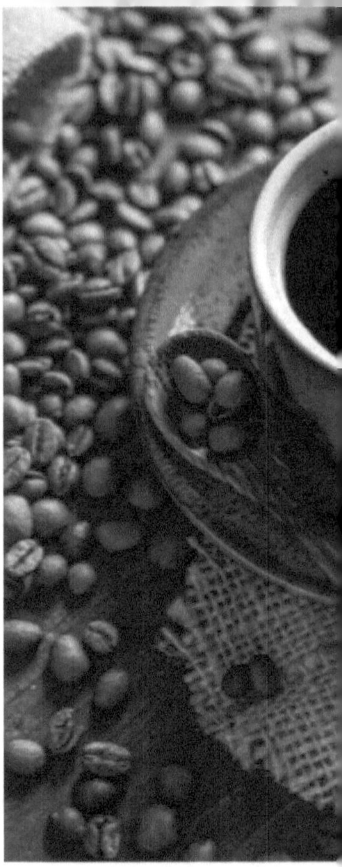
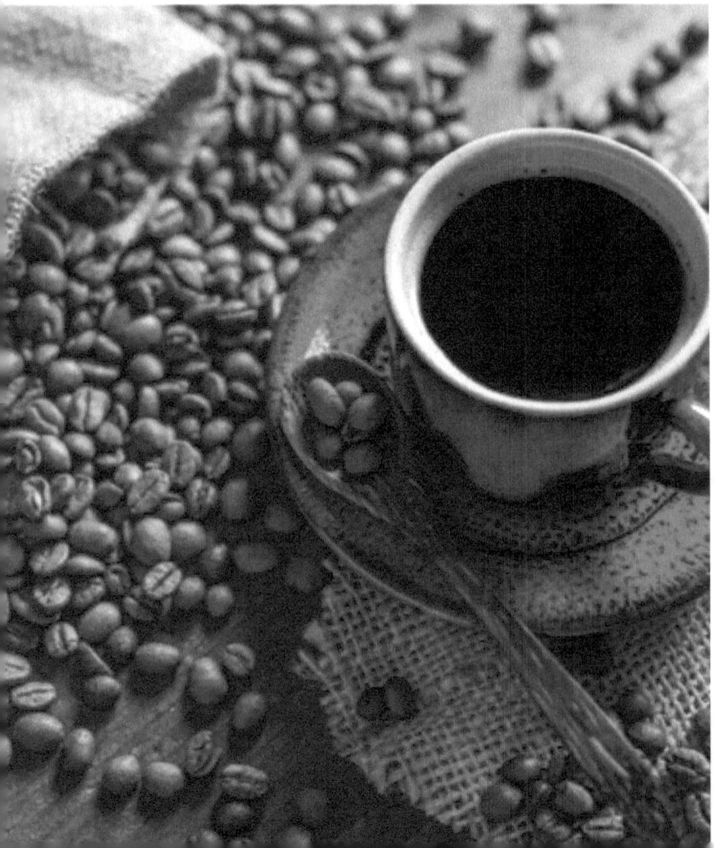
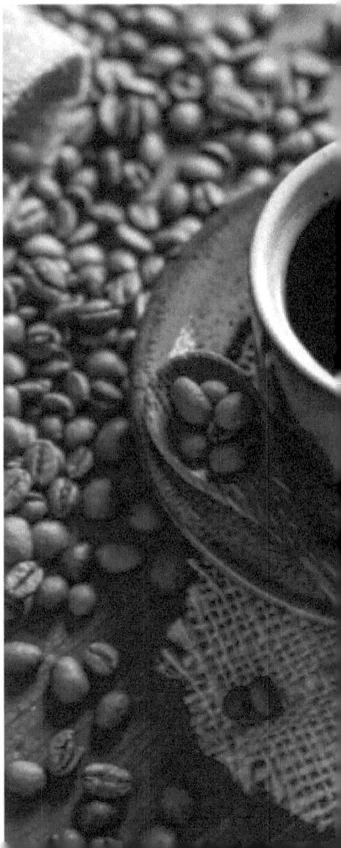

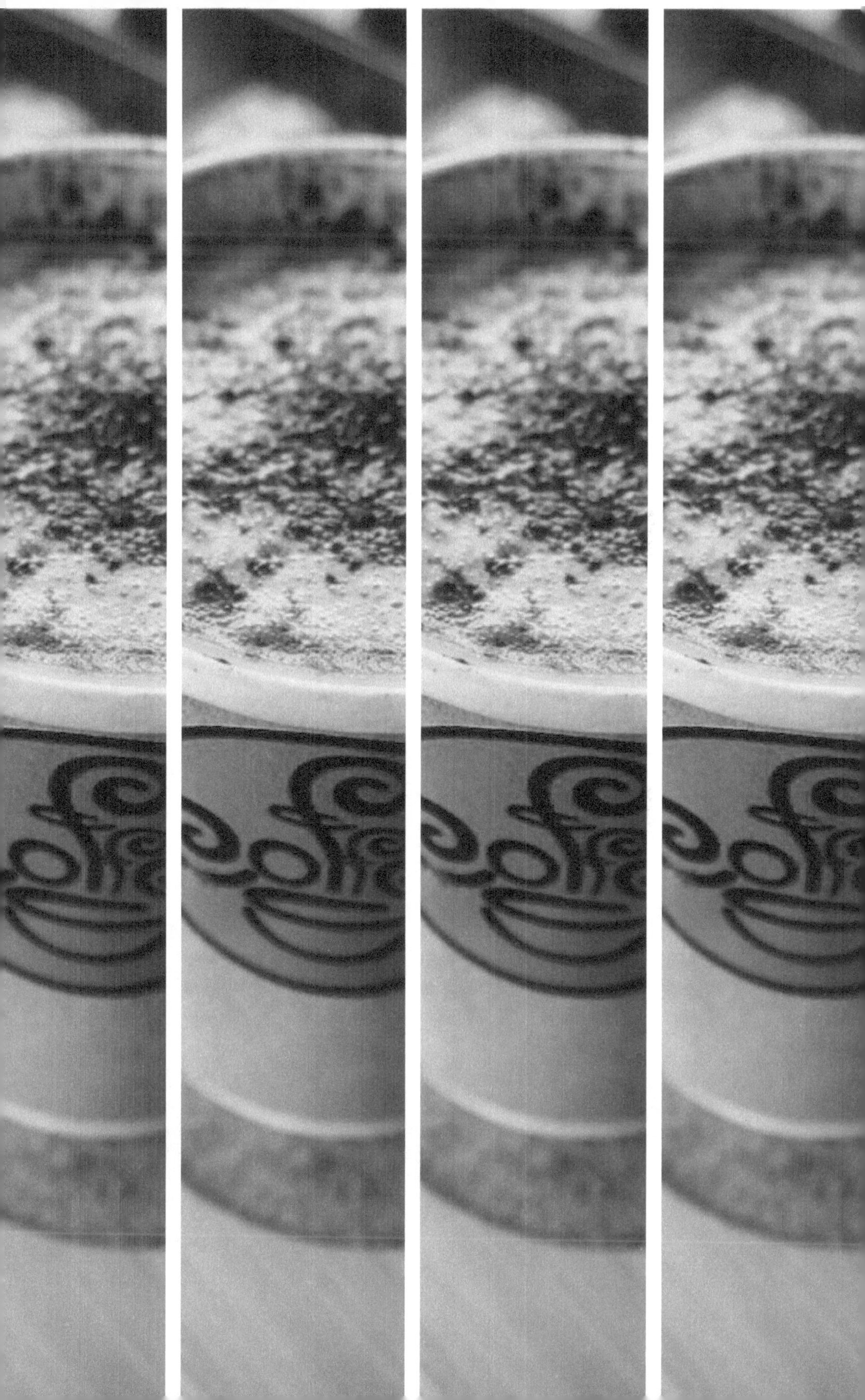

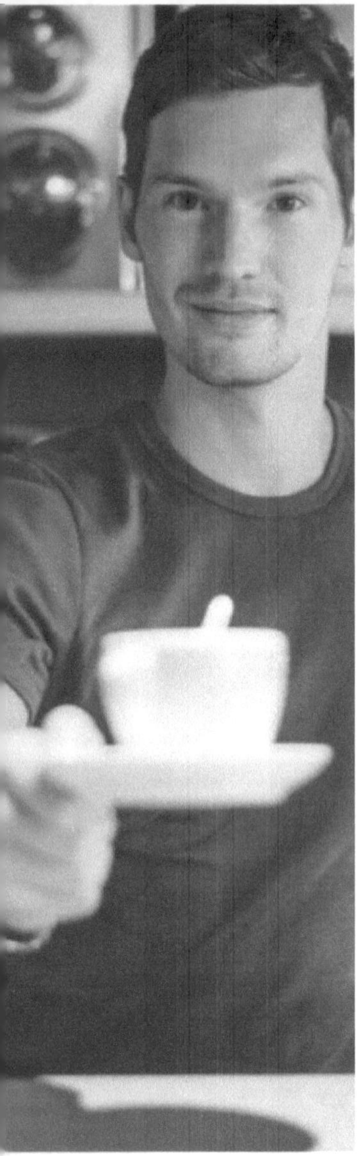
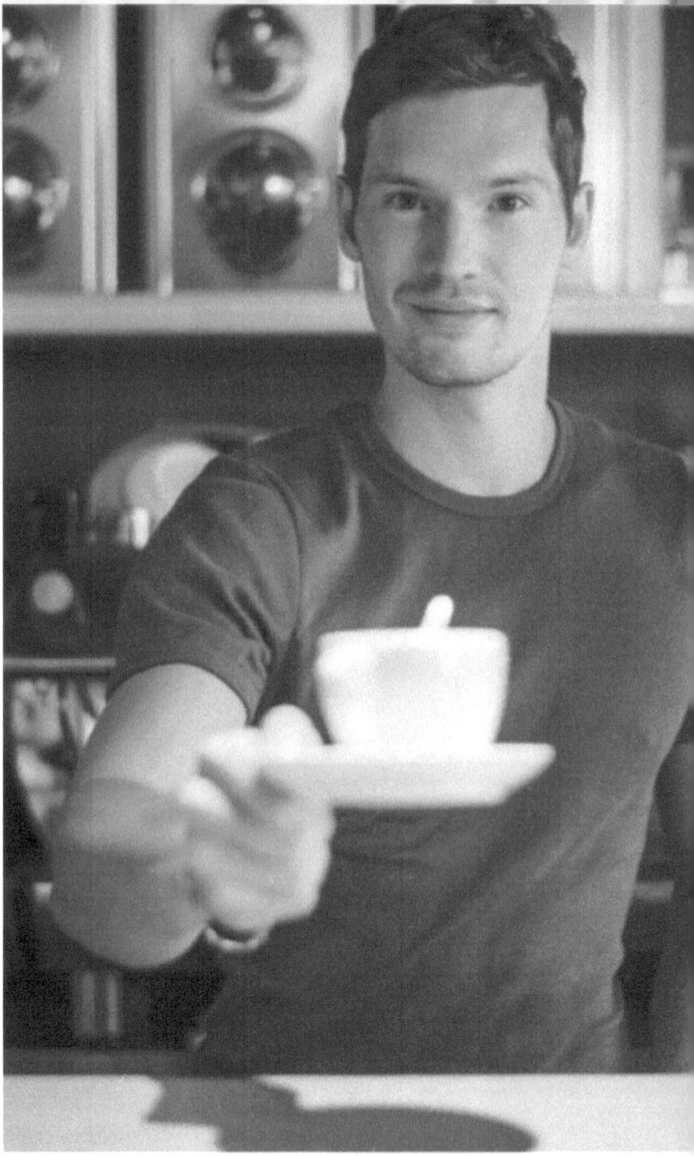
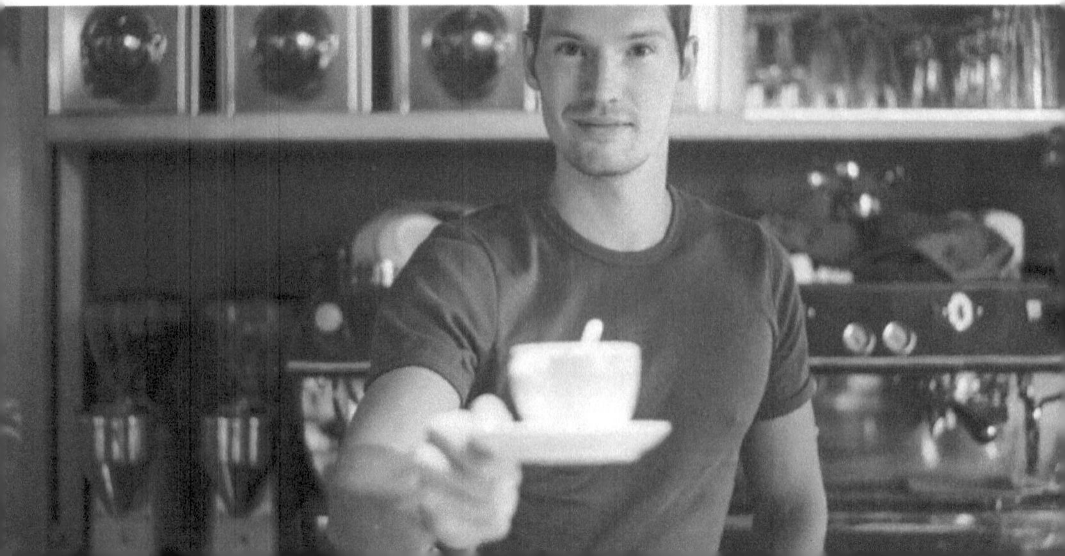

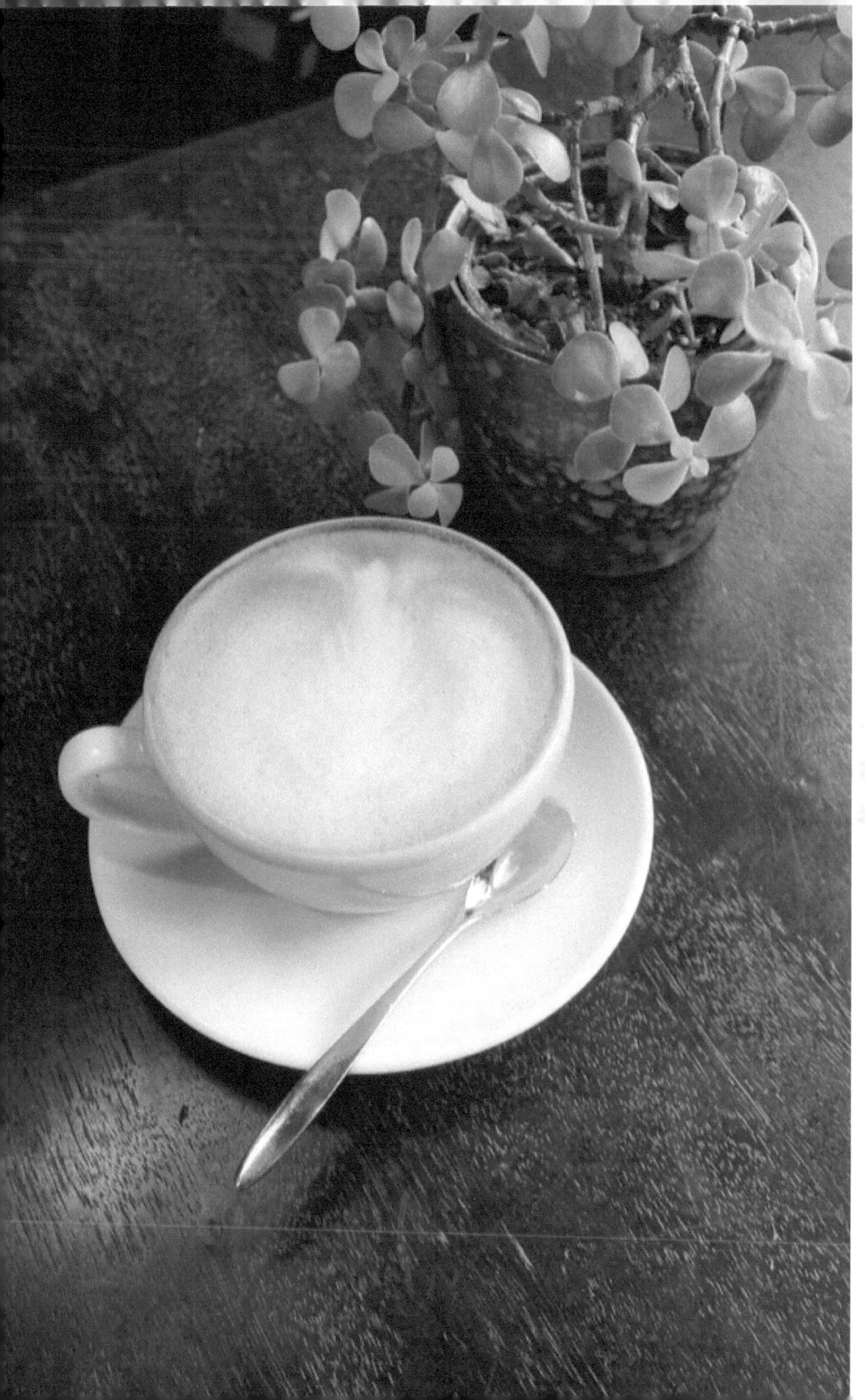

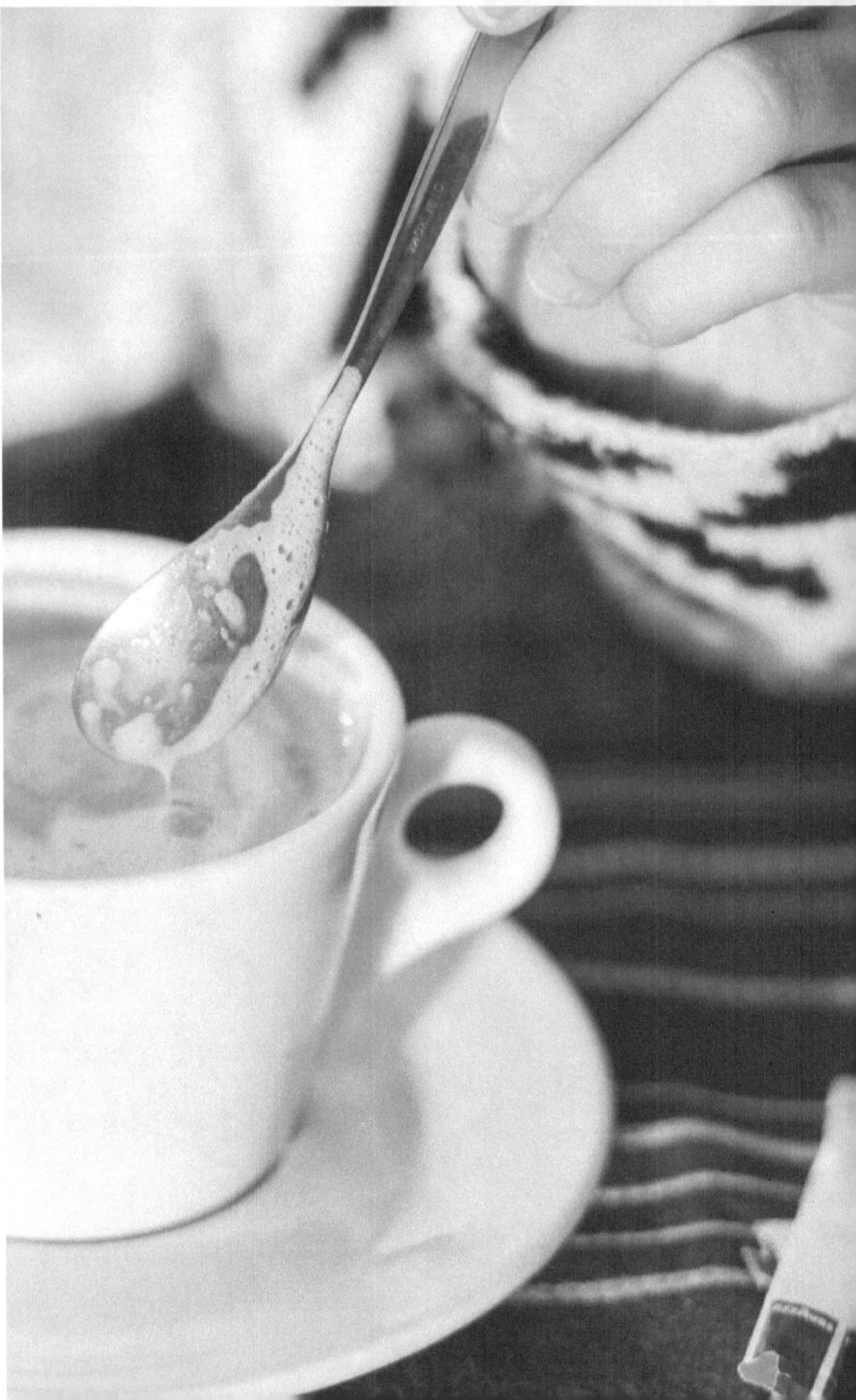

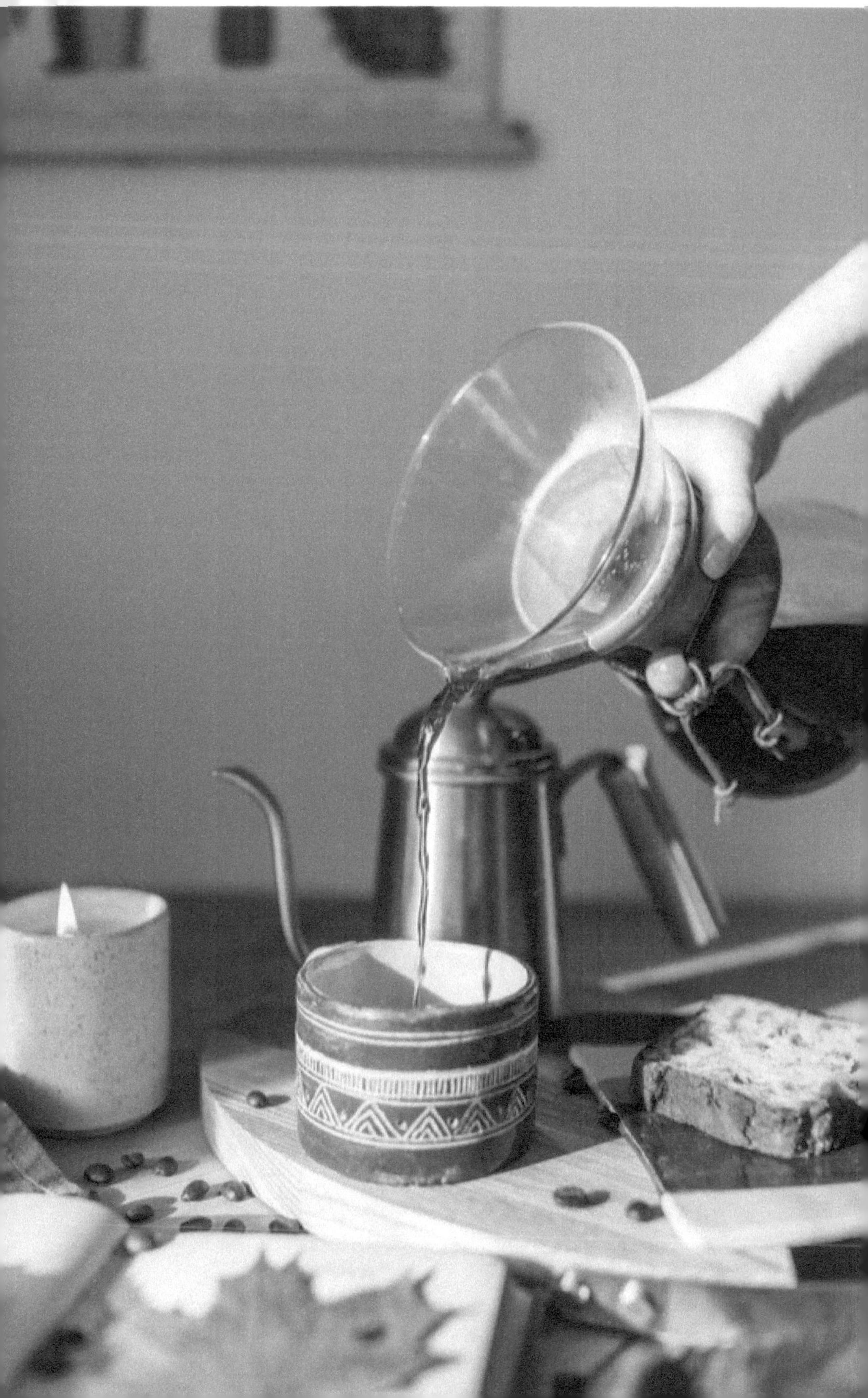

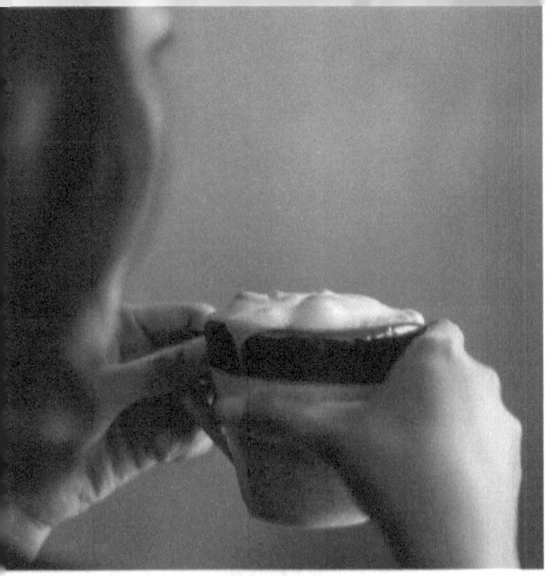
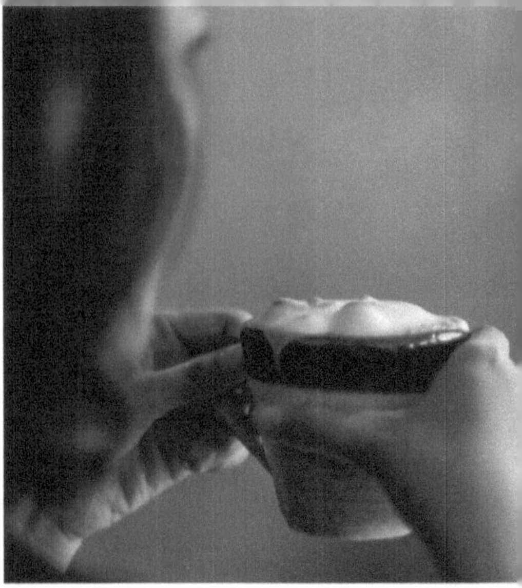
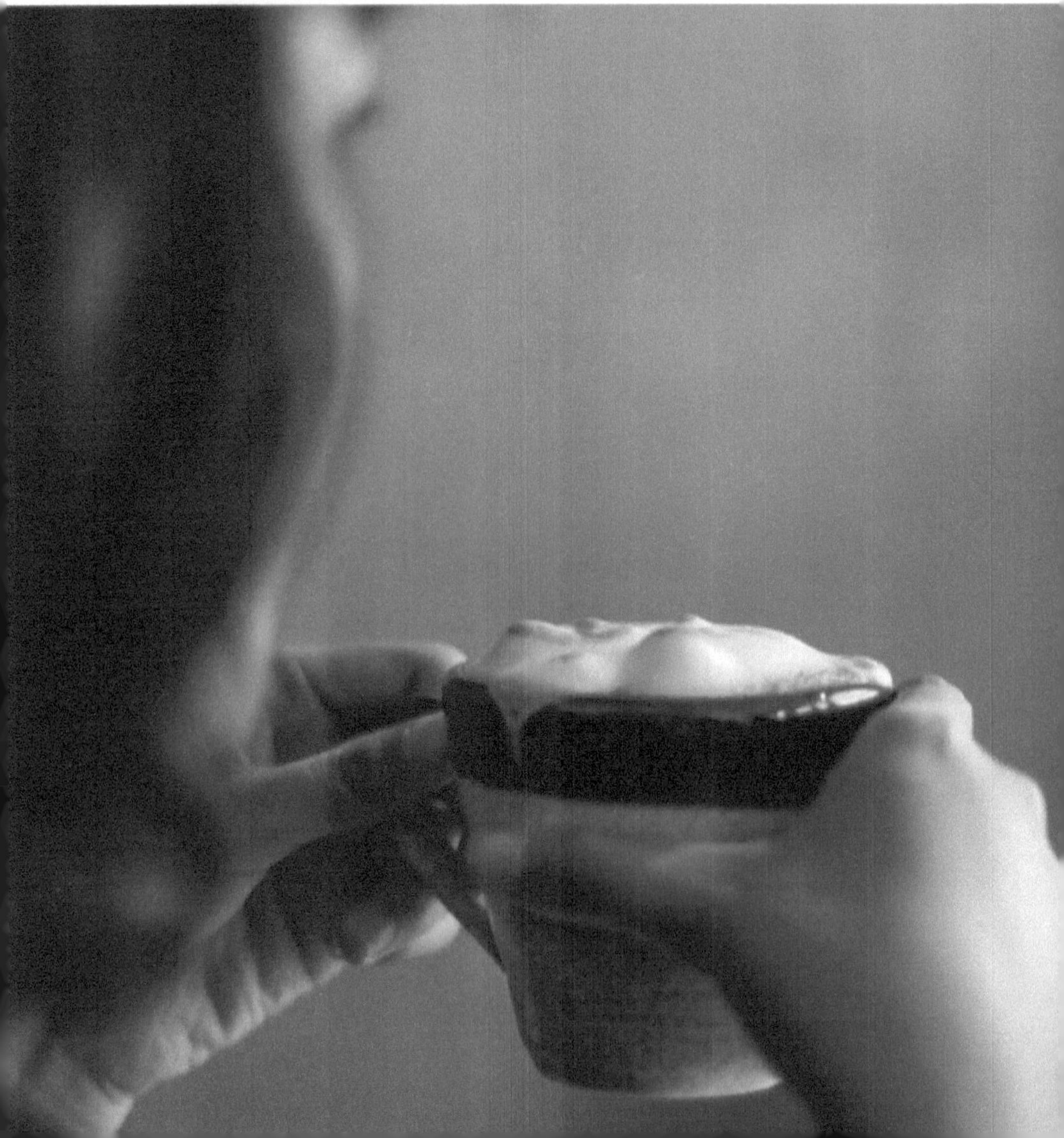

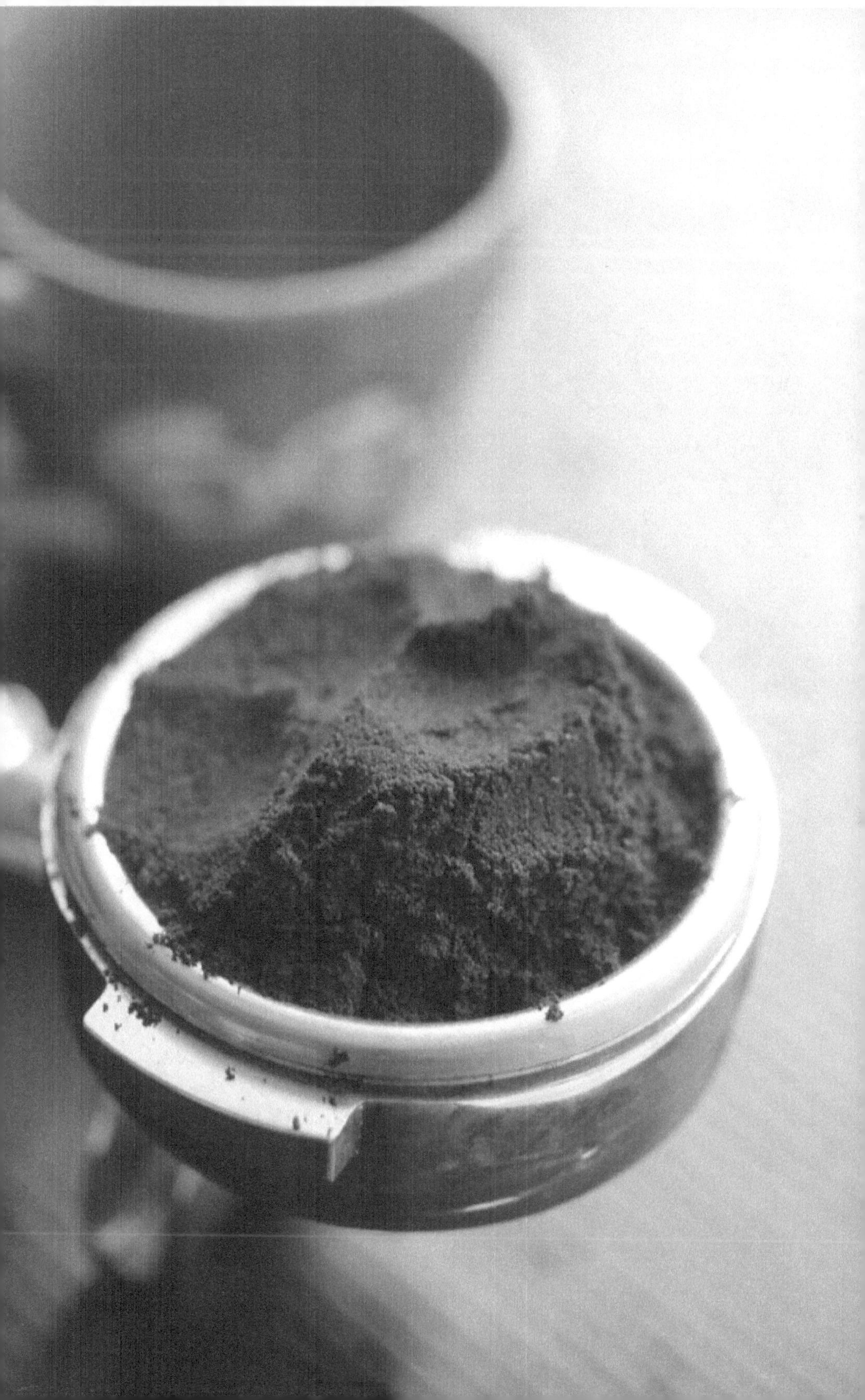

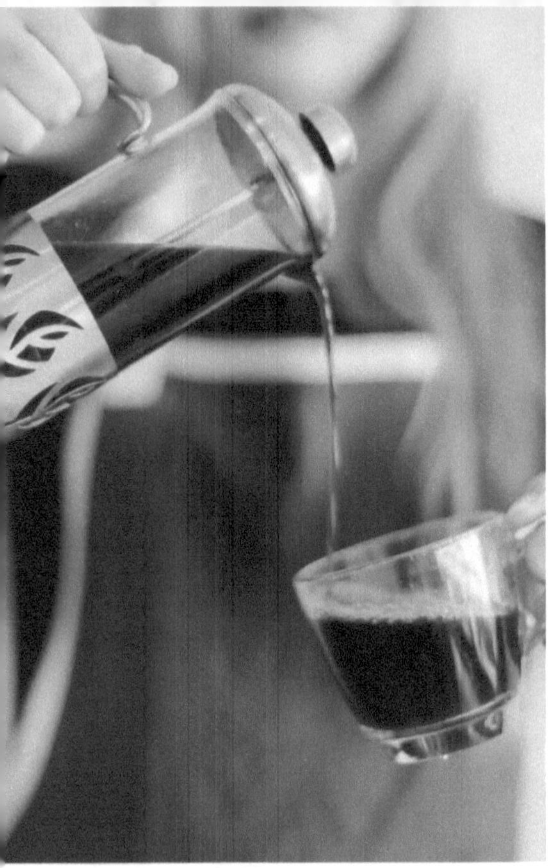
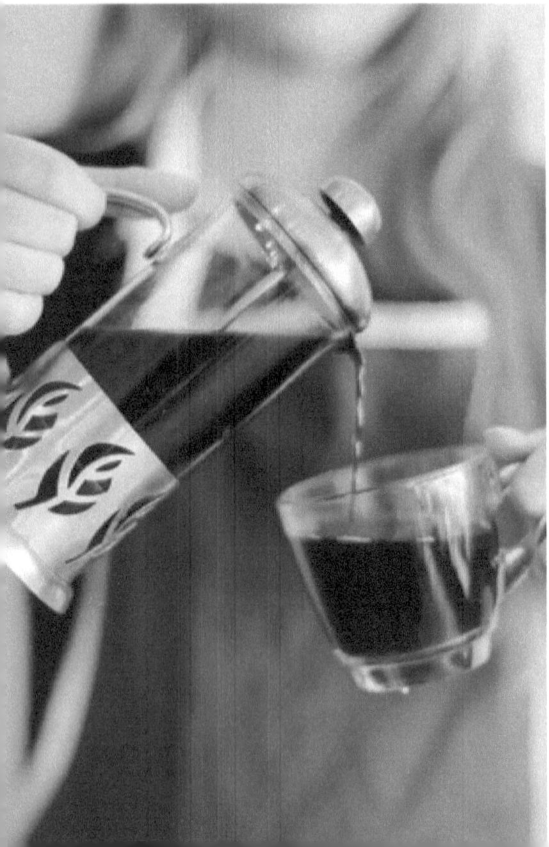
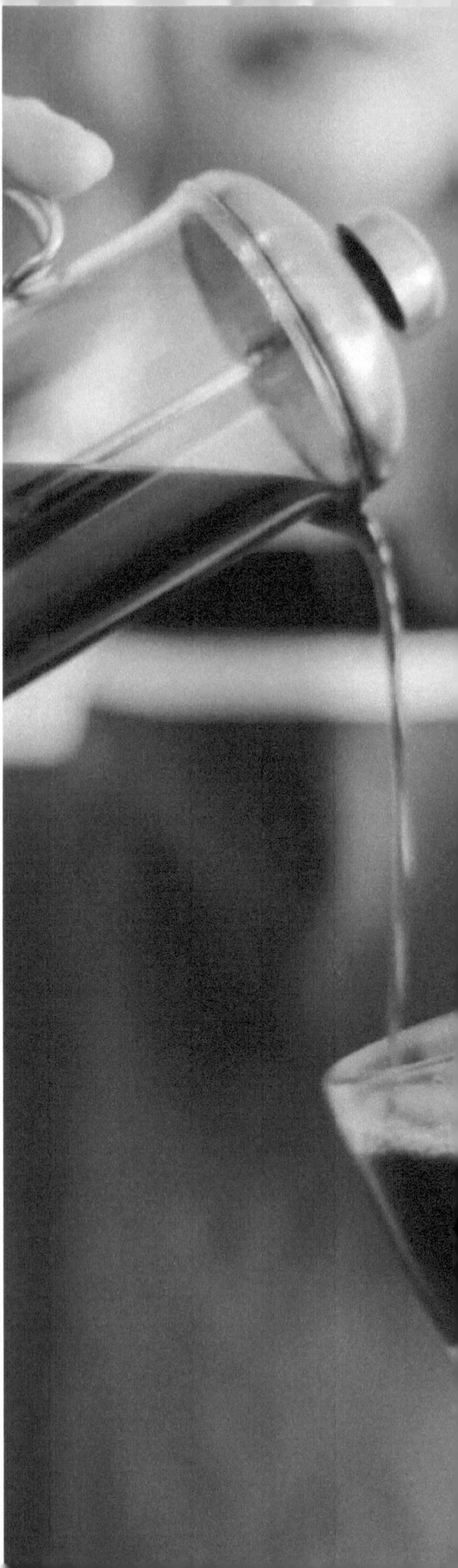

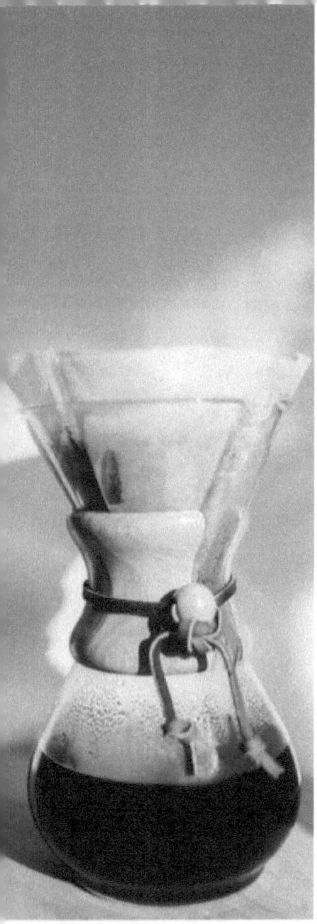
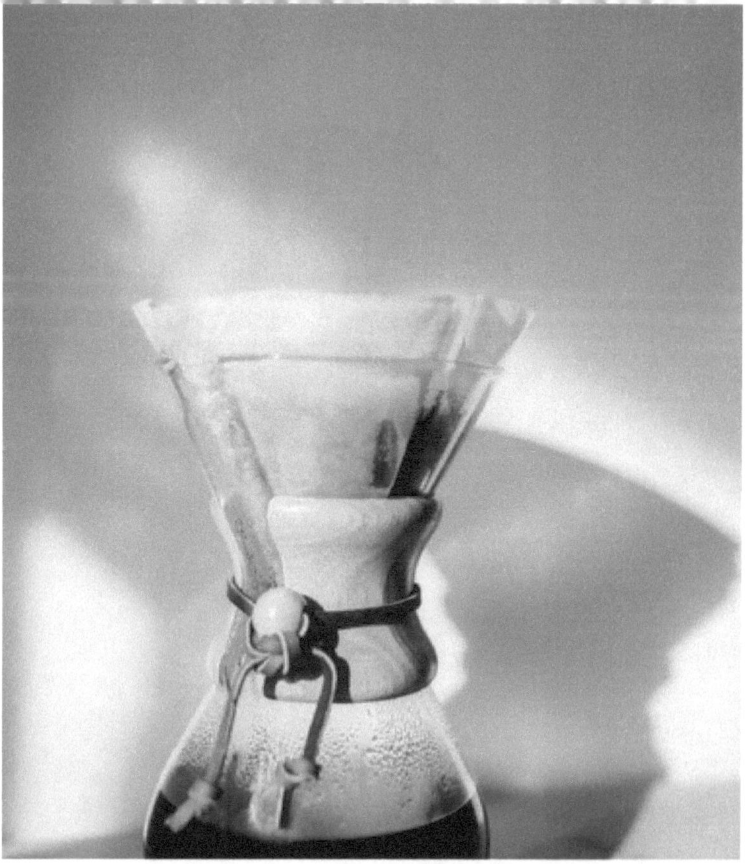
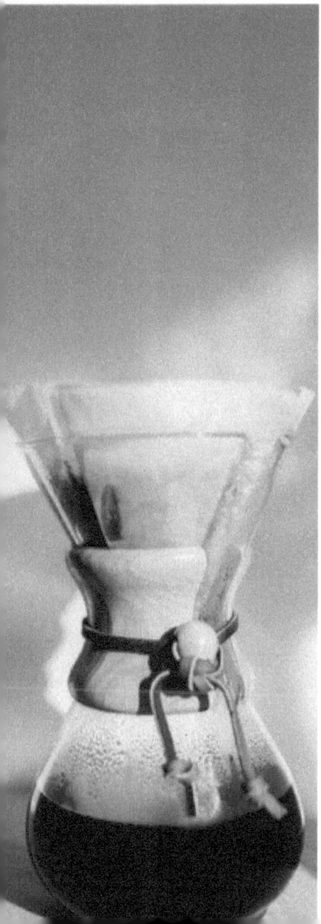
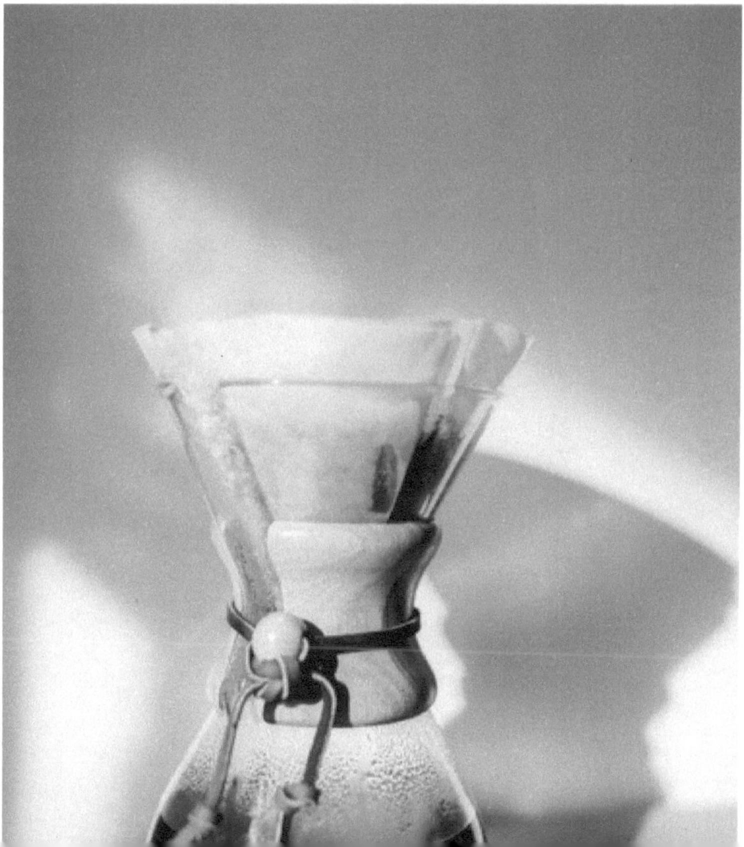

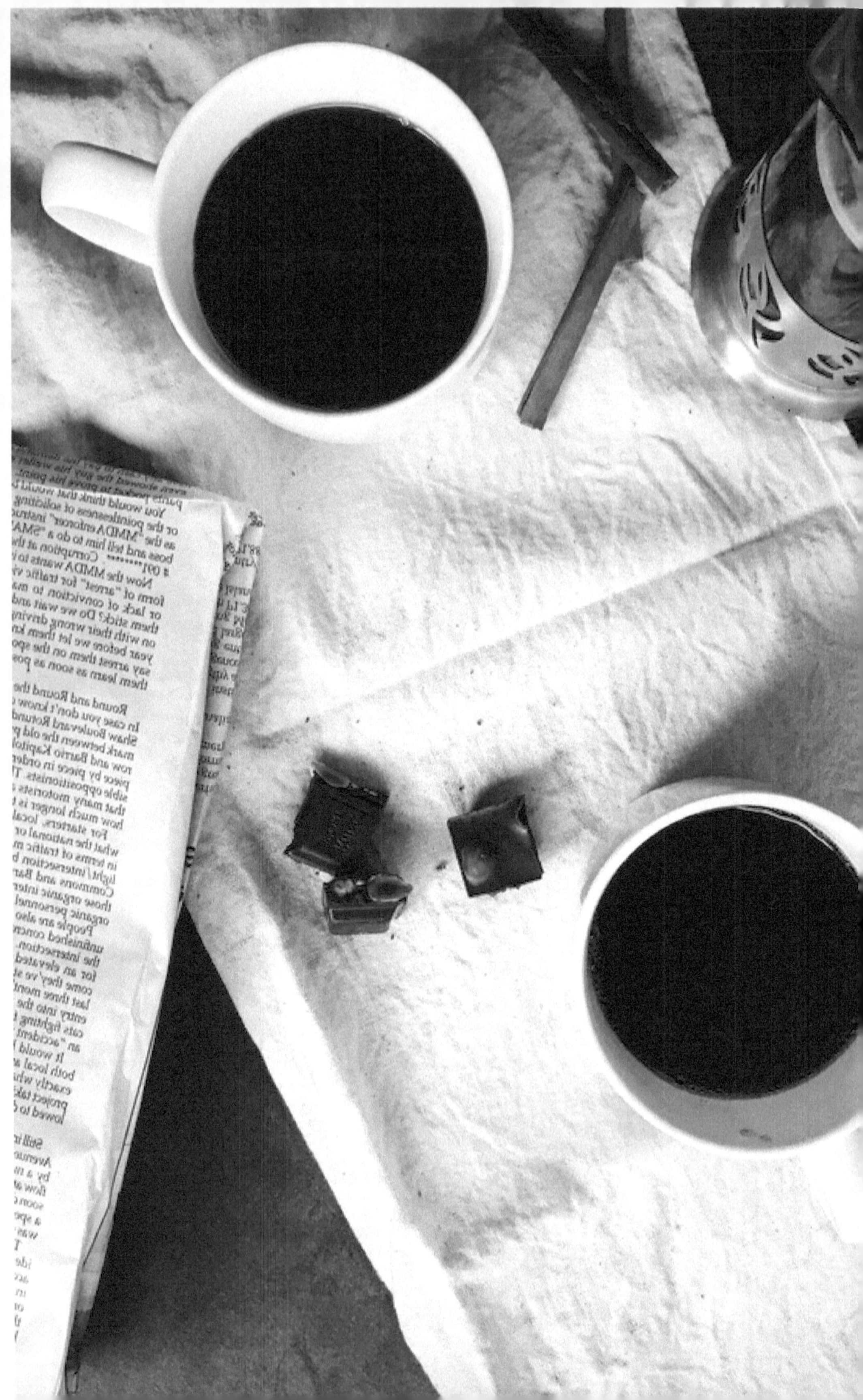

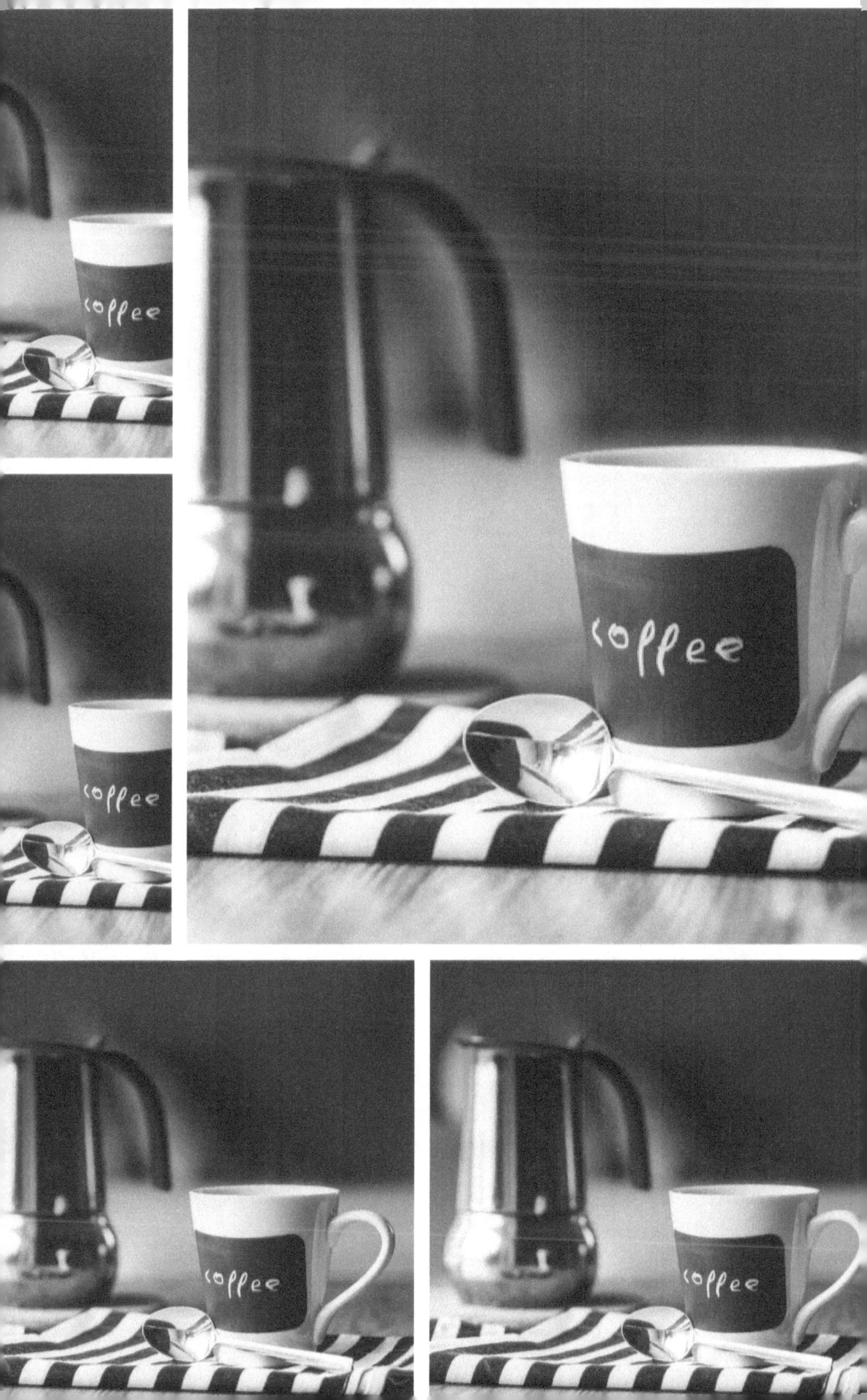
coffee
coffee
coffee
coffee
coffee

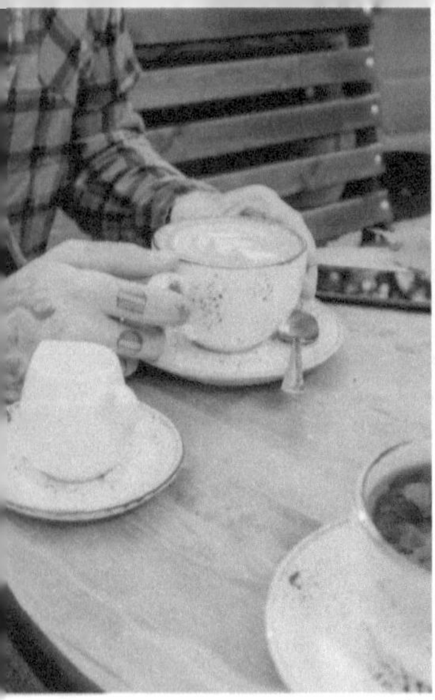
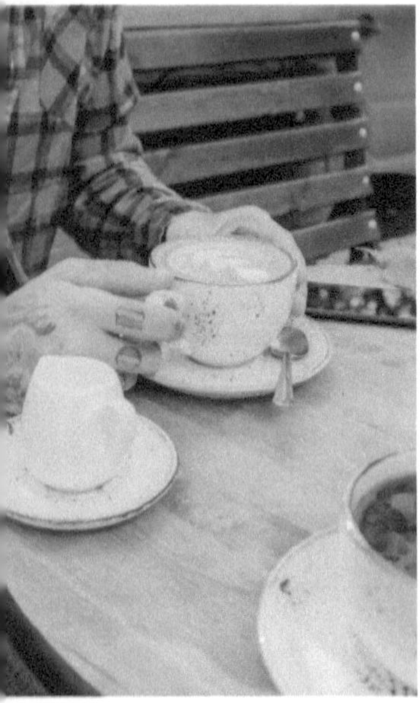
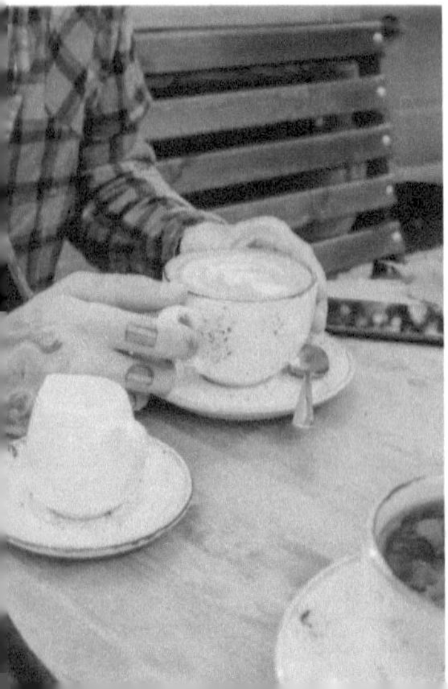
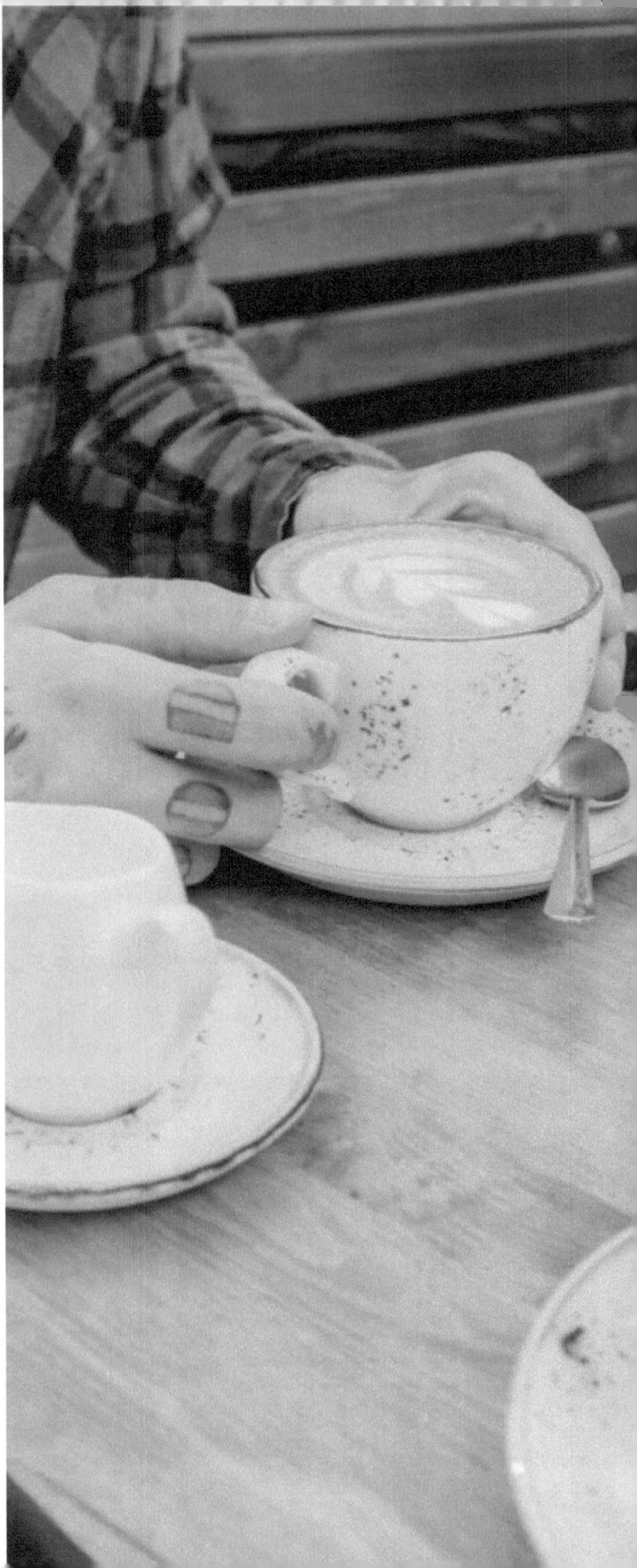

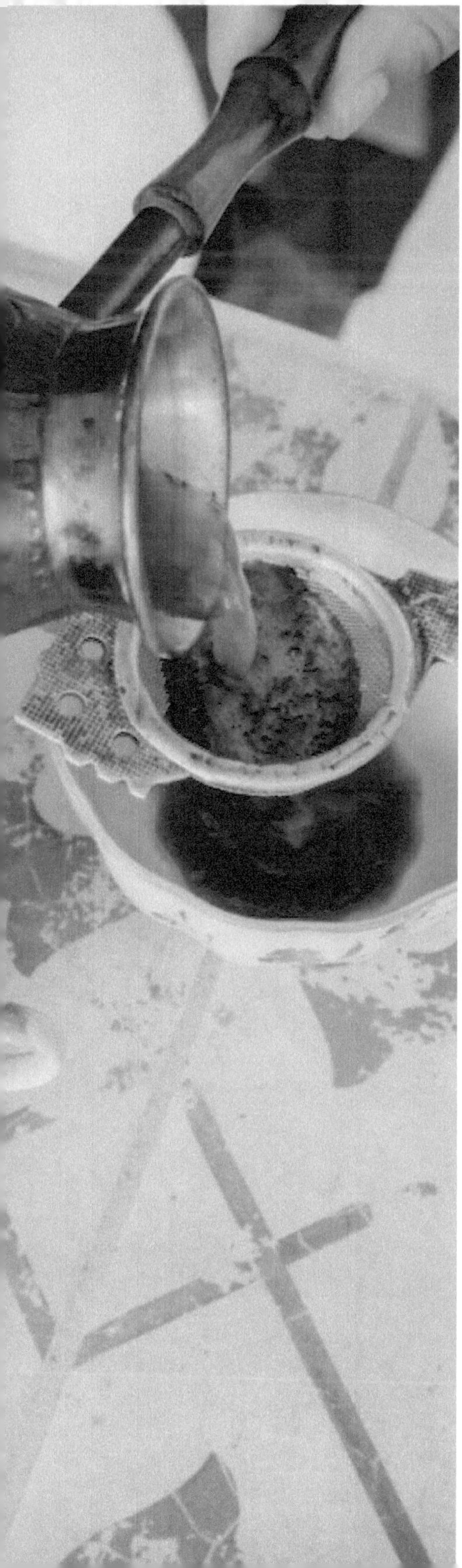

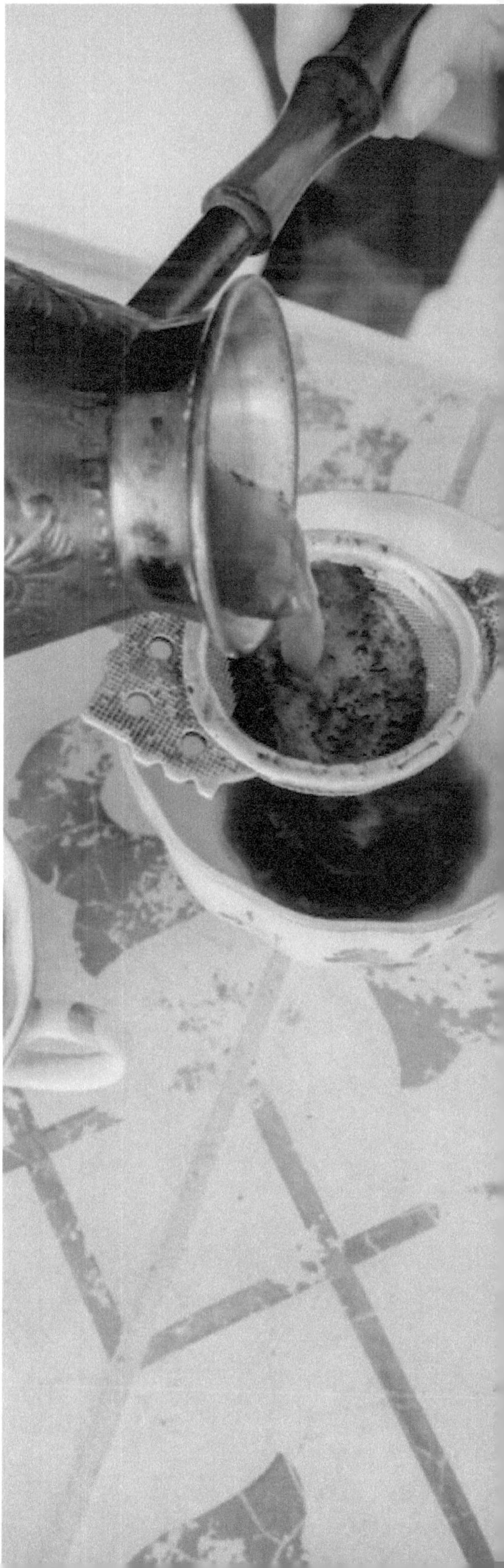

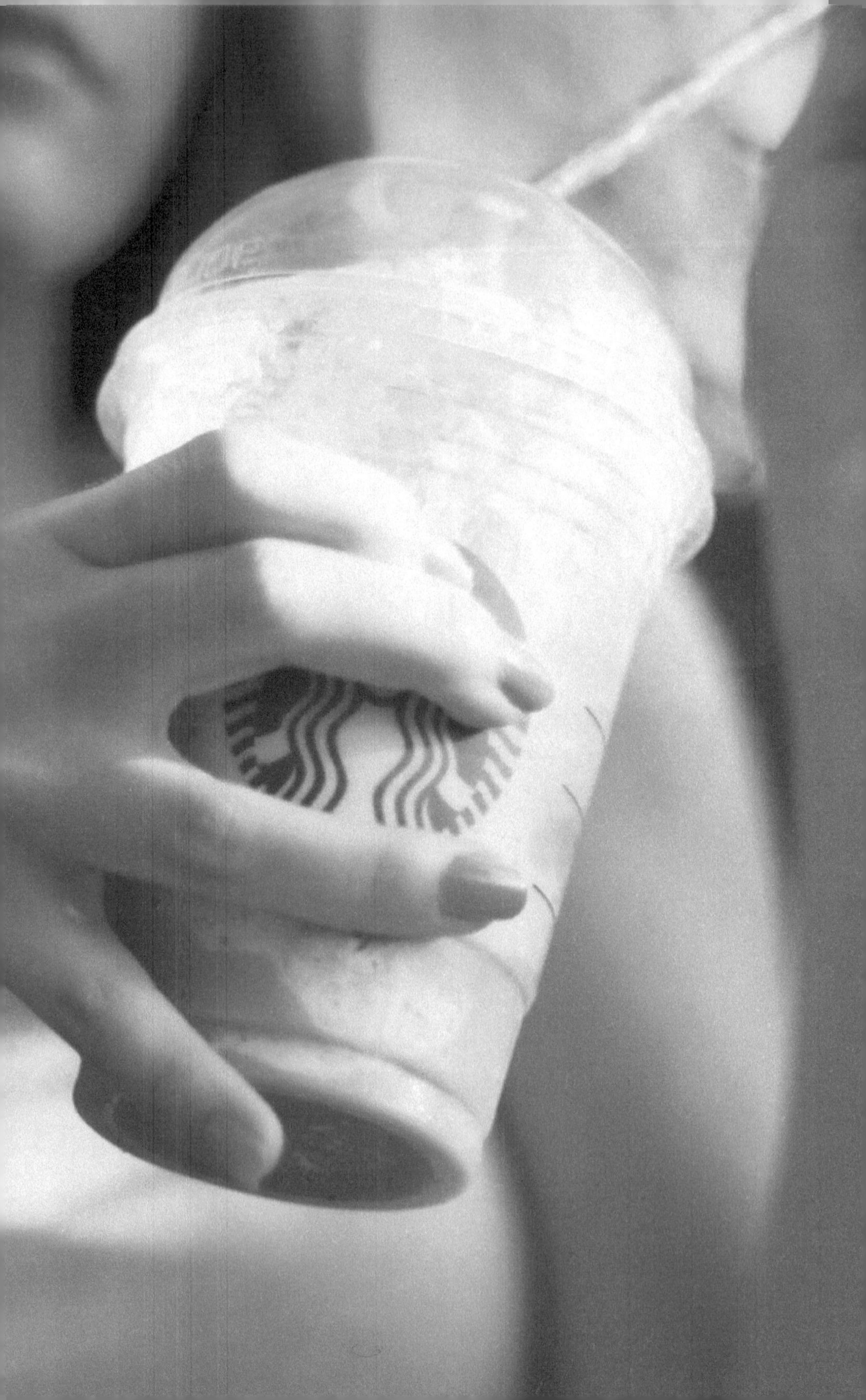

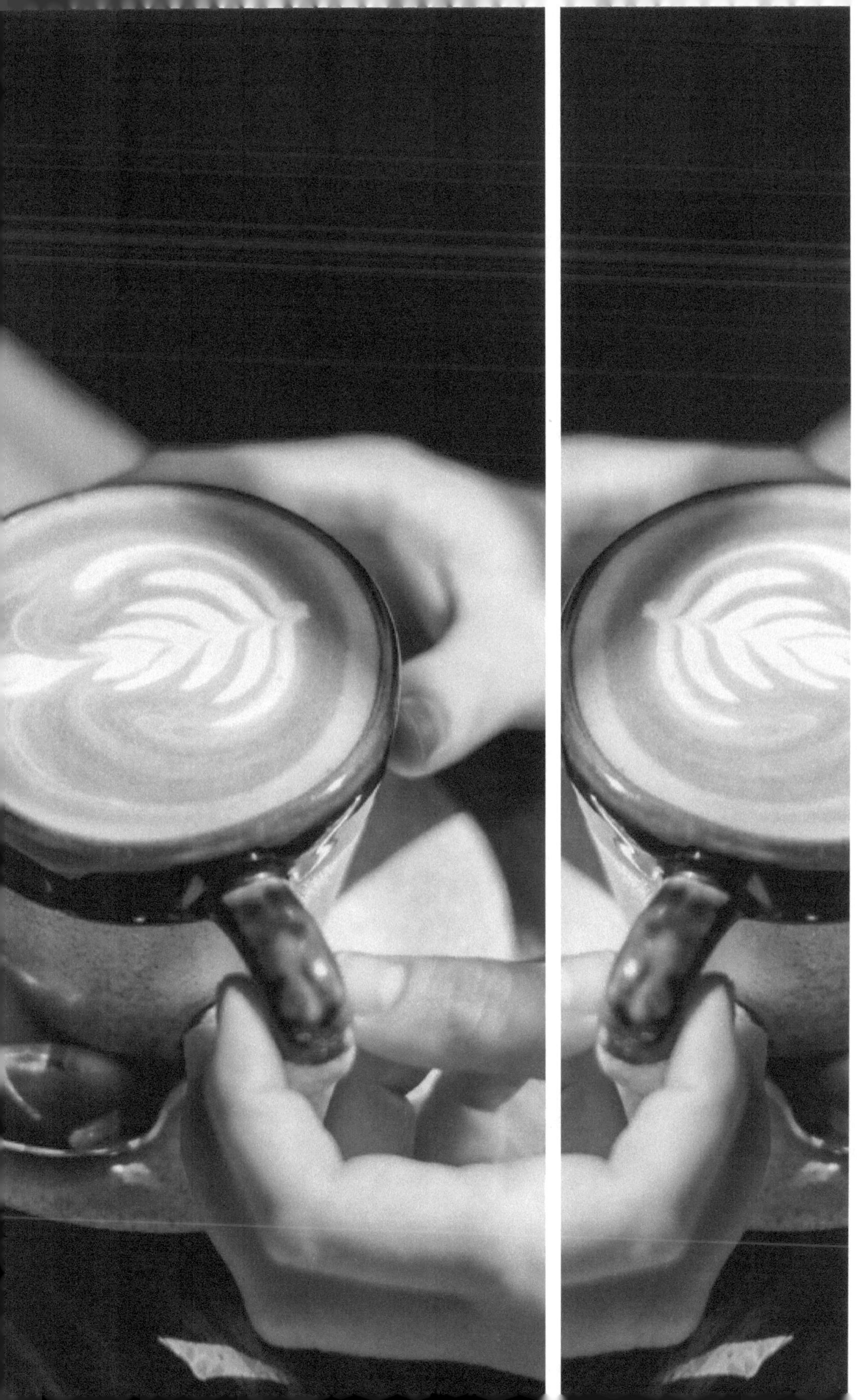

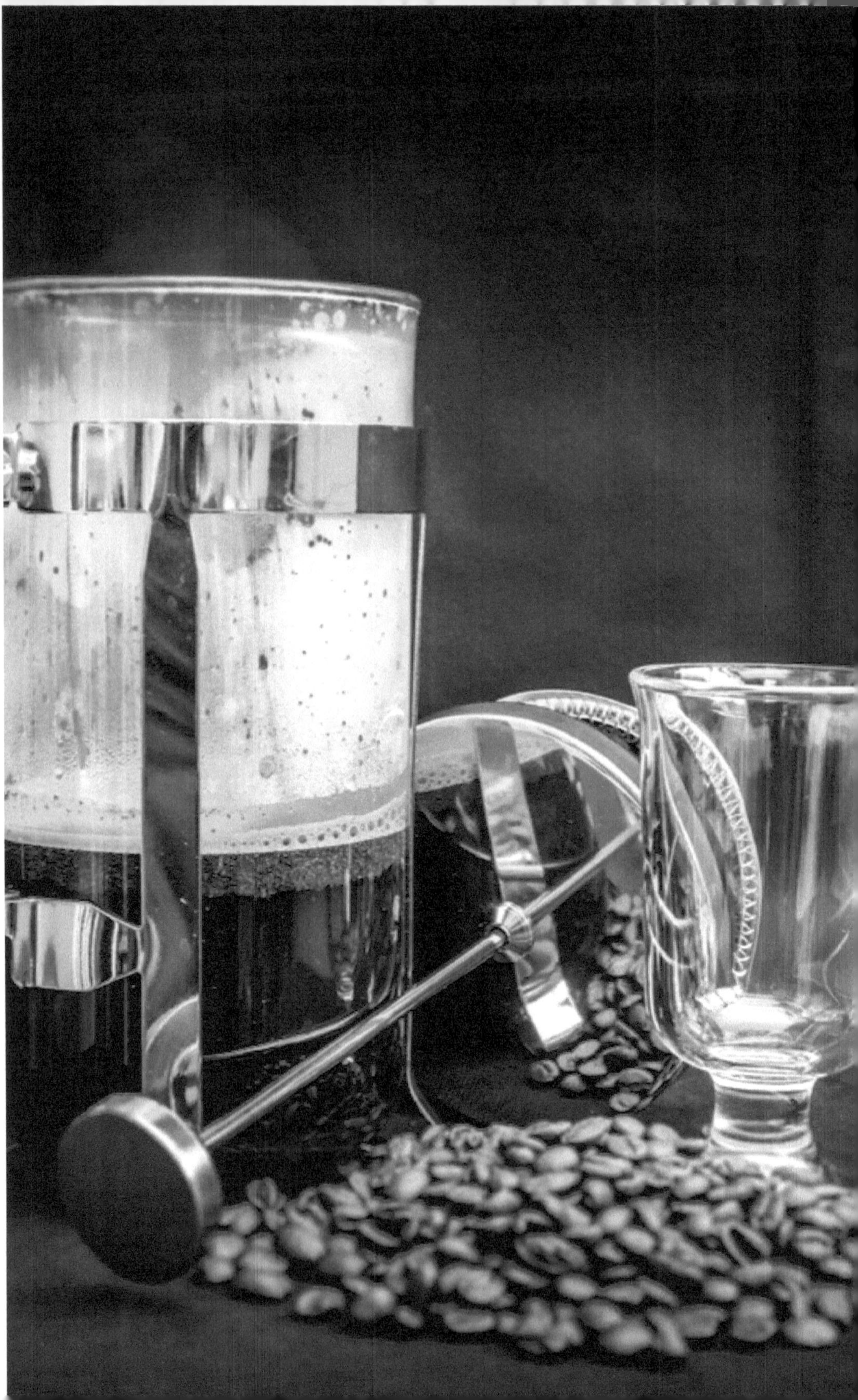

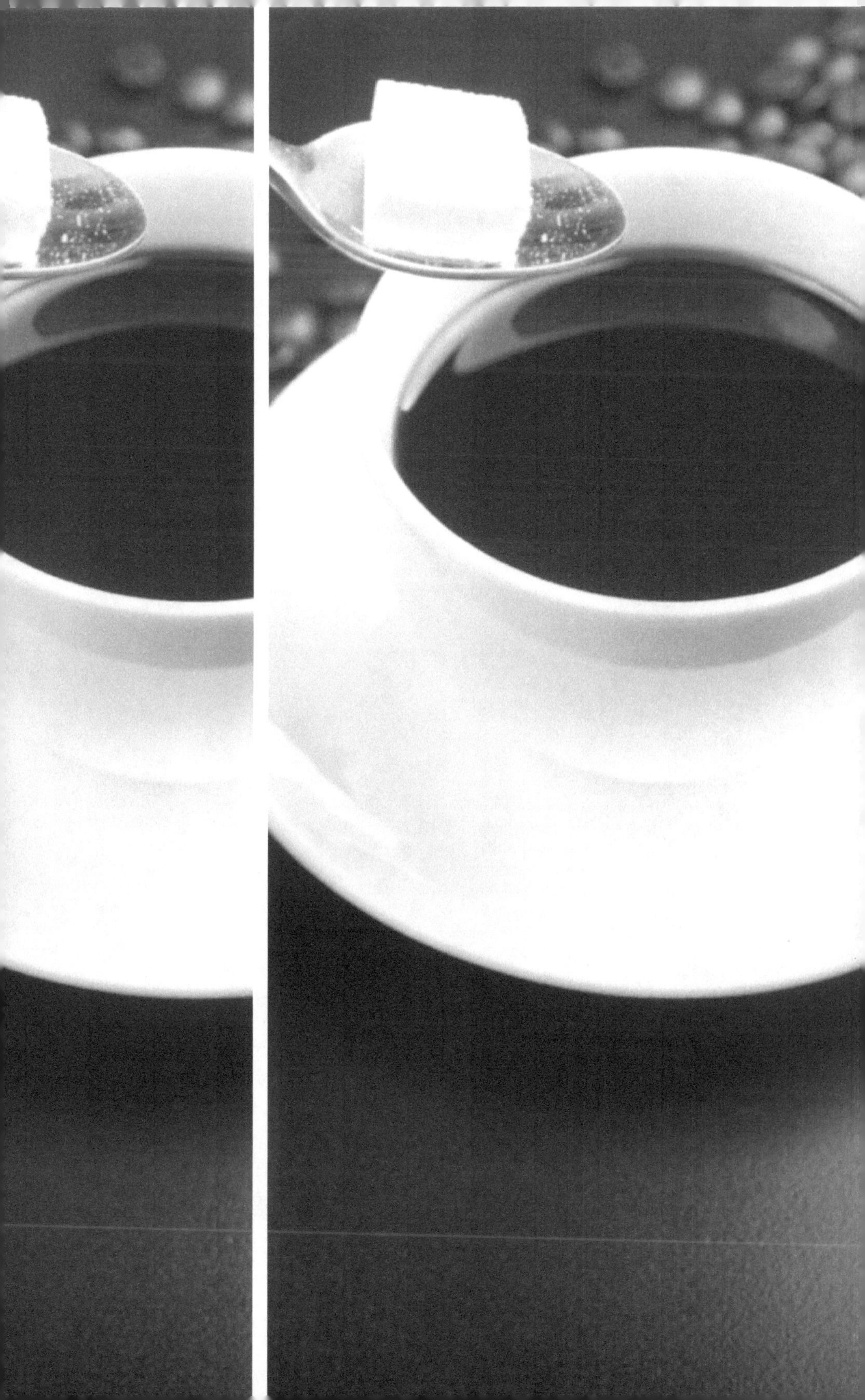

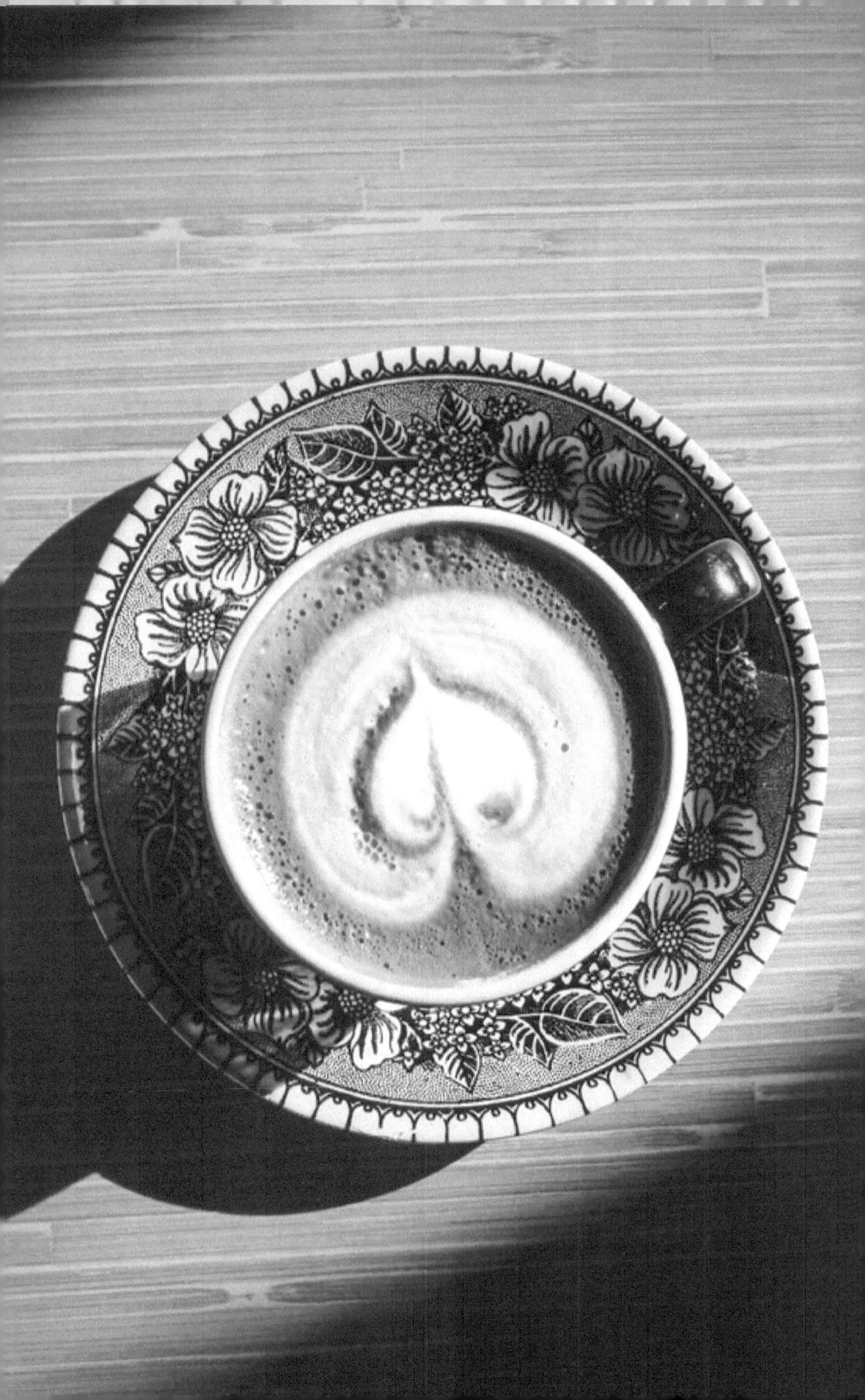

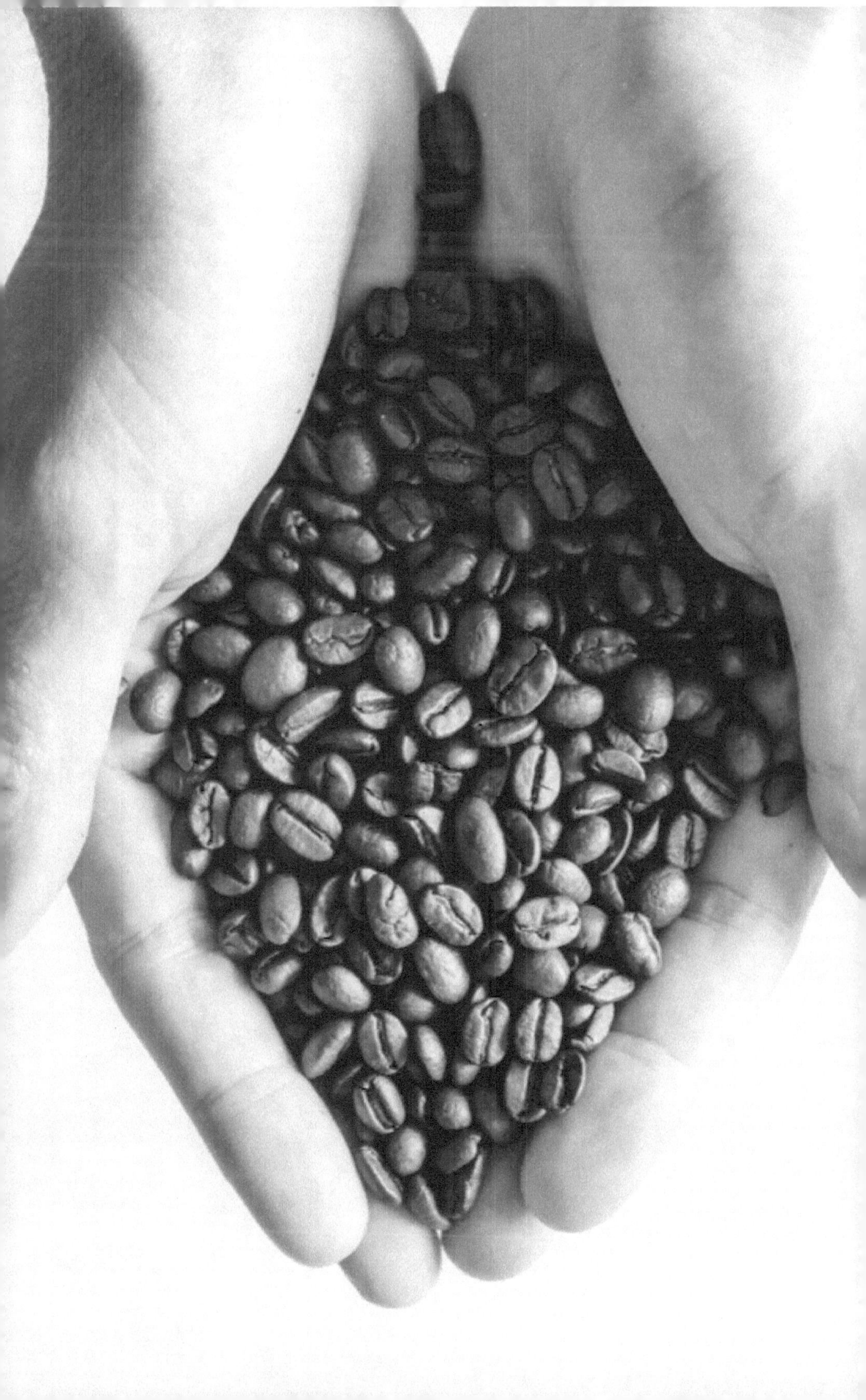

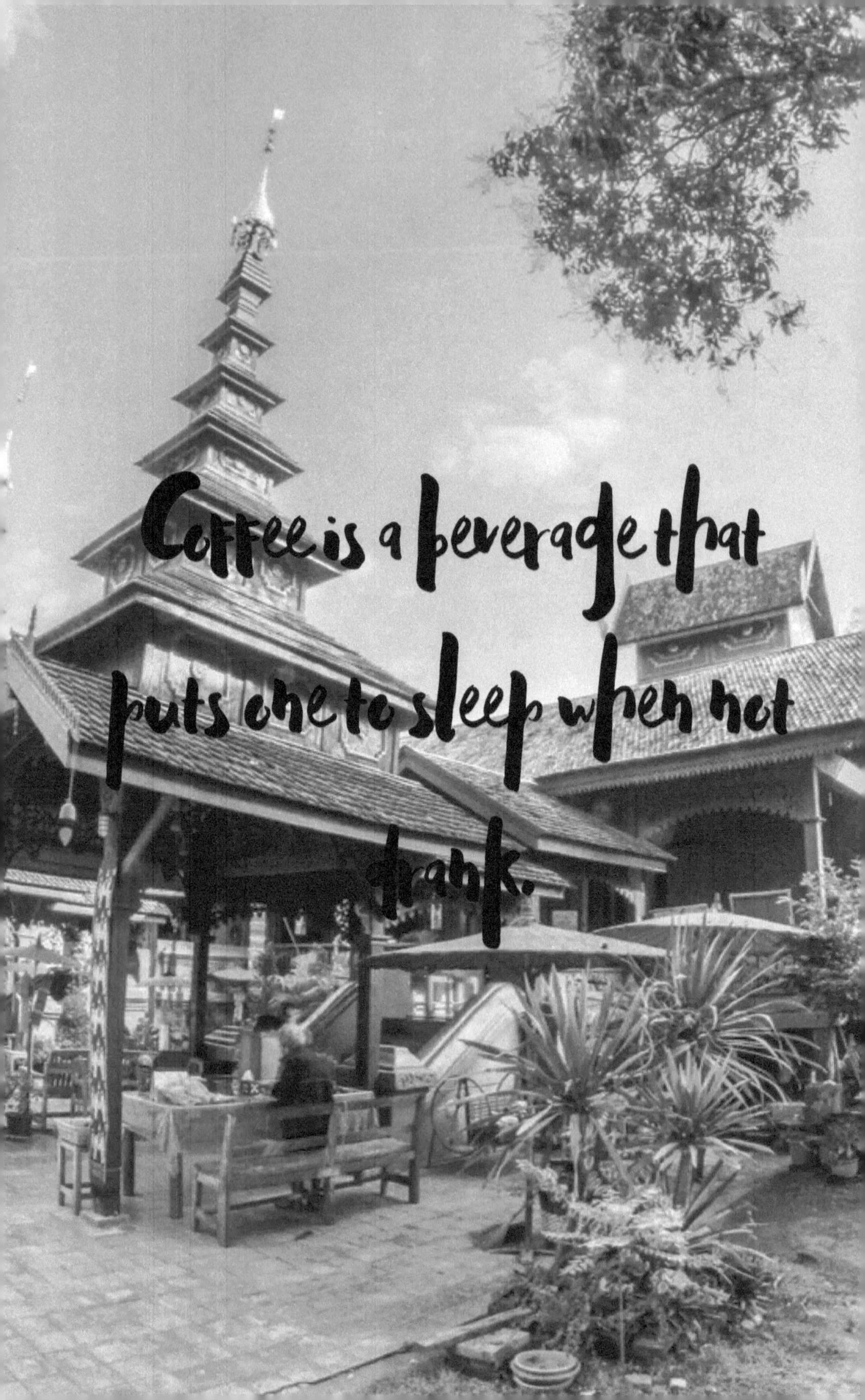
Coffee is a beverage that
puts one to sleep when not
drank.

www.ingramcontent.com/pod-product-compliance
Lightning Source LLC
Chambersburg PA
CBHW021025180526
45163CB00005B/2116
* 9 7 8 0 3 5 9 9 6 7 8 8 9 *